MY AROMATIC KITCHEN

MY AROMATIC KITCHEN

Kille Enna

PRESTEL

MUNICH · LONDON · NEW YORK

AUTHOR'S NOTE

This is a cookbook about AROMA—concentrations and combinations of scents, tastes, textures, and feelings. It is about what I love most, what I spend most of my time on, and what I find most challenging. It is a nakedly honest report about my frustrations and pleasures in finding, retaining, and enhancing the aromatic compounds in food—both out in the garden and inside the kitchen. This is what I think about when I go to bed and what I look forward to when I get up in the morning.

Nothing works alone. We all have sensual relations, even if we don't know it. Feelings and instincts are pure, strong, and measurable qualities. That is precisely what makes aromas so extraordinary and so mysterious—they are things we do not necessarily understand, but have to use our instincts and taste buds to navigate. It is this elusiveness that makes it so fascinating to work with aromas.

Kille Enna

TABLE OF CONTENTS

4   Author's note

8   Aromatic sorcery — Foreword by Chad Robertson

9   Born a star - Foreword by Antony Worrall Thompson

10   The idea behind the book

12   About the aromatic blends — questions & answers

16   Before you start — tools, tips & equipment

24   Application chart for the aromatic blends

CRUNCHY LEAVES & CABBAGES

28   Brussels sprout

32   Cauliflower

36   Bok choy

40   Endive

44   Kale

48   Kohlrabi

52   Chard

56   Spinach

60   How to maximize flavor

WINTER ROOTS

68   Carrot

72   Celeriac

76   Potato

80   Pumpkin

84   Salsify

CAUGHT FROM THE SEA

90   Mackerel

94   Mussel

98   Salmon

102   Shrimp

106   Squid

112   A day in Paris. Talking to Dennis Paphitis

MEAT FROM
THE COUNTRY

118   Chicken
122   Duck
126   Lamb
130   Pork
134   Beef

140   Seasons of plenty

SUMMER
VEGETABLES

144   Asparagus
148   Bean
152   Cucumber
156   Fennel
160   Leek
164   Onion
168   Zucchini
172   Radish
176   Tomato

182   Adventures in my Swedish country garden

THE PANTRY

186   Chickpea
190   Egg
194   Flour
198   Lentil
202   Rice
206   Dried fruit
210   Yogurt
214   Seed

220   Edible flowers — precious moments

RIPE FRUITS

226   Apple
230   Peach
234   Melon
238   Pear
242   Quince
246   Rhubarb

250   Homegrown luxury

PICKED
FROM THE
BERRY BUSHES

256   Gooseberry
260   Raspberry
264   Strawberry
268   Black Currant

274   The essentials of herbs & spices
281   Menus for the four seasons

285   About the photographs
285   Thank you
286   Recipe index
288   About the author

AROMATIC SORCERY

A few years ago, my dear friend Kille announced that she was done with cooking, done making cookbooks. She had spent decades cooking and writing books as a chef, all the while obsessed with aromatics from around the world—spices, dried flowers, citrus, and herbs from near and far. Kille decided to focus purely on capturing and preserving the aromas of botanicals, making her own edible aroma extracts, as a very personal project and new business venture many years in the making.

The process proved an especially arduous journey—perhaps the most difficult of her professional life. But in this world of botanical aromatics, Kille found herself profoundly happy and very much at home. Her obsessive drive to find the highest quality organic aromatic edible flavors and to synthesize them into powerfully evocative blends had unexpectedly opened a pathway back to the kitchen.

From this period, a focused new perspective on cooking had emerged, one built from both worlds in which Kille lives—the practical and the spontaneous—and embracing fantastic worlds of flavor and aroma that come together here with accessible and affordable basic ingredients. Using a chef's approach to sourcing and creating edible aromatics, Kille has assembled fifty formulas—some dry like spice blends and some wet like pastes, dressings, and marinades—with examples of how to enliven even (and especially) the most basic of ingredients into incredibly delicious meals. Gently informed by the seasons, and with a foundation built more on vegetables than meat and fish,

her book begins with clear directions to start the journey and maps to explore ingredients in different combinations.

Kille has famously cooked from her own garden in the Swedish countryside for many years and for many book projects. While that's still true here, My Aromatic Kitchen is also a bold return to cooking and a culmination of decades of flavor synthesis. Kille's philosophy shines a light on simple ingredients and techniques. She's written a confident guidebook presenting ways for us to make extraordinarily flavorful dishes with ease.

Clear, focused, and with a distinct point of view, Kille's book is generous in a way that is both playful and highly informed. Her seemingly effortless genius puts a smile on my face as I smell and taste these aromas and flavors. It's much like the smile that comes through in the way Kille shares her vision to cook simple daily food on her own practical terms. This is the food I want to eat everyday.

My Aromatic Kitchen is Kille's temple food from the garden: fresh, nourishing, and with a master's hand of aromatic sorcery shifting our focus back to simple ingredients with powerful, healthy flavors.

Chad Robertson
Co-founder of TARTINE Bakery & TARTINE Manufactory,
San Francisco

BORN
A STAR

Many years ago, Kille Enna, a mere slip of a thing, flew down to London for an interview as a young chef, and flew back the same day. I had never seen such enthusiasm from one so young, and I haven't seen it since. She surprised me with a spirit and passion well beyond her years. One part of her interview has stayed with me. She said: 'I love swimming with fishes—they fascinate me—but more importantly, I want to know how to cook with them. I have chosen you to teach me.' Wow, that was deep. I immediately offered her a job—brave, I know—but I had this inner feeling that Kille was going to achieve great things. She didn't disappoint.

There was no stopping Kille. She was like a fish in a mountain stream, gracefully swimming upstream, and overcoming any obstacle thrown in her path. She took no prisoners, occasionally failing to understand that not everybody has her passion. She couldn't and wouldn't tolerate inefficiency, ignorance, or the inability of others to love their food. This caused ripples on the water and she made several enemies, mainly those jealous of her outstanding talent. I was never one of those enemies; Kille's talent excited me. I had hooked the fish, but never wanted to land it. I wanted her to swim and swim, learning, loving, and living for food. She had a talent that outshone all those around her, and yet in chef terms, she was still a 'baby'—but what a baby!

There were times when I wanted to 'father' Kille, to tell her to be patient with others less focused than she, and to concentrate on her own amazing talents rather than brood over the inadequacies of others who worked with her, but that's easier said than done. I had to give her 'gardening' leave in the true sense of the word, to let her loose on the plants and trees with which she had a better affinity. Only then, at one with nature, could she unwind, let loose, and return to serenity. But then she'd be back in the driver's seat once again, ready to push herself to the limit, ready to seek new challenges. I have never seen, and probably never will see, another chef like Kille. She became my youngest ever head chef. Now she's moved on to greater things. This book and her previous books capture her extraordinary abilities, her amazing imagination, and her understanding of the world we live in.

Kille Enna was born a star, and continues to be a star, totally at one with nature, totally at one with food, and totally at one with life. I will always be sad that I lost her to the bigger world, but I will always be proud that she chose to start her adult life with me.

Antony Worrall Thompson
TV chef, author, restaurateur, London

THE IDEA BEHIND THE BOOK

This is my tenth cookbook, but for me, it is much more than that. It is something new and different: an attempt to use simple aromatic blends to create unique and sensual experiences in the kitchen. First, let me explain why it turned out this way …

I have no helpers in the garden or in the kitchen. I take care of everything and do everything myself. It's a fairly simple equation and one that brings me great joy, but in terms of time, it doesn't work. I am professional, efficient, and focused when I work, but if you're going to cultivate a garden and cook everyday, while running a business, and all with a satisfactory end result, then something has to change. So that's what I've done! I rarely freeze anything—that has never been my style. I simply don't have the heart for it. I would much rather eat all the ice cream I've just made than freeze any that's left over, because there is simply nothing like freshly made ice cream. In fact, I have also

COMPLICATED TECHNIQUES ARE NOT NECESSARY WHEN YOU HAVE A RIPE KEY INGREDIENT AND AN AROMATIC BLEND

stopped preserving fruits and vegetables. In the past, I would spend weeks bottling and canning all my garden produce in jars, making tomato ketchup and mustard, pickled melon skins, ginger beer, preserved lemons, gherkins, sauerkraut, pickled herring, apple butter, and all sorts of jams, often adding large amounts of sugar and vinegar to make them durable. The idea of being able to relive summer flavors, when the ground is frozen solid and it is bitter cold outside, is wonderful and very sensible and I admire those who do it, because they bring pleasure to others. But every year, I found the mere thought of having to get through all that, alongside my work, enormously stressful. The absurd thing is that it all has to be harvested and prepared in late summer, which is my absolute favorite time in the garden. I hardly had time to be out there to experience it, but instead spent my time indoors. The last year has been different, and that has been liberating.

My favorite cuisine is street food, because it's served quickly, and is fresh and highly fragrant. If I eat in a restaurant, I order lots of different starters as my main course, and want them brought simultaneously. I've always been interested in mixing and comparing combinations and concentrations when I eat. On the other hand, I also enjoy putting my fork into a big, juicy, medium-rare steak, with just the perfect sauce and no accompaniments. That makes me full and satisfied in a completely different way and I don't need to eat meat at all for the next few weeks.

I don't drink alcohol, which isn't a hardship, but a decision I made twelve years ago. It's a way of staying focused on what I'm eating and experiencing. I've actually never drunk wine at dinner. It can cause confusion and create a distance that makes it harder to enjoy the natural aromatic substances in food. Wine is a full meal to consume in itself, as it has its own set of incredibly complex aromatic compounds. If I were to drink wine at dinner, I'd probably do it before or after the meal to have the time and the tranquility to fully experience the wine's aromatic potential.

In light of all this, it is clear that I place extra-high demands on the seasoning of food. So, instead of creating yet another cookbook, with a classically structured collection of recipes, I've done the exact opposite. I've taken out all the noise, and cut it right back to the bone. I've spent an enormous amount of time figuring out how to best show you all the things I care about, both visually and in terms of taste. The result is fifty aromatic blends and each aromatic blend is combined with a key ingredient, which becomes a dish. I chose to work with fifty ingredients—the key ingredients—that we all know and use, in one way or another. They are easy to get hold of and aren't expensive.

The key ingredient that's paired with the aromatic blend has been chosen to best illustrate the potential of that individual blend. Moreover, the aromatic blends must also be suitable for combining with ingredients other than the ones highlighted in the book. So, the majority of the aromatic blends must, for example, be robust and stable enough to be used on the stove instead of in the oven as it says in the recipe. The aromatic blends also solve the problem of lack of time that I and everyone else must deal with, no matter how experienced and efficient we are in the kitchen. And if you're like me, you don't want to compromise on scent or taste.

Over the past year, I've had many sleepless nights, because I have prepared and developed recipes that are completely different from those I usually create. I have eaten differently—more aromatically and more simply. I've gone out to the garden and dug up vegetables that were in season, cut spinach, and picked fruit and berries. In the kitchen, I dropped all the complicated techniques. I've given the key ingredients the minimum amount of preparation, and kept away from complicated knife skills. Why? Because they are not necessary when you have a ripe key ingredient and an aromatic blend, a blend that includes all kinds of textures, nuances, fragrances, and flavors—everything that makes carrots, apples, potatoes, leeks, or salmon suddenly taste of so much more. Because together an aromatic blend and an ingredient create a meal that is both simple and refined. My aromatic blends are tools that will add a distinctive scent, flavor, and texture to your cooking. They are easy to make and easy to use. Enjoy!

INSTEAD OF CREATING YET ANOTHER COOKBOOK, WITH A CLASSICALLY STRUCTURED COLLECTION OF RECIPES, I'VE DONE THE EXACT OPPOSITE

ABOUT THE AROMATIC BLENDS— QUESTIONS & ANSWERS

ARE THE AROMATIC BLENDS EASY TO MAKE?

Yes, they are easy to make and easy to use. You don't need professional tools to make them, nor do you need to master complex techniques or have advanced knife skills. That's the whole idea of this book. Some aromatic blends take just a few minutes to prepare, and most of them can be made within half an hour. Others are boiled, and so take a little longer, while a few are used as marinades for meat and fish, such as in gravlax (p. 98), and therefore need a few days before the dish can be enjoyed.

WHAT DO THE AROMATIC BLENDS CONSIST OF?

All the aromatic blends contain different textures, nuances, fragrances, and flavors. Some aromatic blends are juicy pastes that are made, for example, from fresh ginger, garlic, or turmeric. Others are dry mixtures made from freshly ground spices, or a combination of seasonal fruit, herbs, flowers, and vegetables. Aromatic blends can be raw or cooked, coarsely chopped or blended. Sometimes the preparation can be done in a bowl, by simply mixing all the ingredients together; other times the ingredients must be chopped, grated, or dry-roasted before being used. And, for a few of the aromatic blends, all of the ingredients go in a pot and are boiled on the stove.

WHAT DO THE AROMATIC BLENDS TASTE LIKE?

The aromatic blends follow the changing of the seasons. They supply fresh and sour flavors, and are highly fragrant, without being strong. The acidity comes from different ingredients, including ripe fruits and vegetables, unfiltered apple juice, drained yogurt, and dried berries. Many of the blends feature various fresh and dried flowers, which can make the overall taste experience more feminine and poetic. And then there are the aromatic blends that draw inspiration from near and far. This comes from a well-traveled life in which I have visited most of the continents, and have lived and worked in several of them. The aromatic blends can be adapted to your own taste by using more or less of them, or by replacing one key ingredient with another.

WHERE DO YOU DESCRIBE THE INDIVIDUAL AROMATIC BLENDS?

The scent and taste of each aromatic blend is described in the recipes, under Character. I have separated the aromatic blend and the dish, because the aromatic blends can be used in dishes other than the featured one. I describe the aromatic blends in words that are light, dreamy, and fairly diffuse. My intention is to promptly call forth a mood, so that you know what to expect if you use the blend with another key ingredient. Remember that the aromatic blends are not dishes in themselves, though many of them taste delicious. Each blend is a tool that will add a distinctive scent, flavor, and texture to your cooking. Further down the page, in the introduction to the recipe, you can read about what the dish itself tastes like.

THE AROMATIC BLENDS FOLLOW THE CHANGING OF THE SEASONS

CAN THE AROMATIC BLENDS BE USED WITH OTHER KEY INGREDIENTS?

Yes. This is described in each recipe, under Variations, while in the 'Application chart for the aromatic blends' (p. 24), you can see even more possible combinations. The key ingredient used with each aromatic blend has been chosen to best illustrate the potential of that individual blend. For this reason, I advise you to follow the recipe to the letter, before you try replacing the key ingredient. Then you will know what the aromatic blend tastes like, its strength, and its possible limitations. By

now, I know my aromatic blends very well. I use, for example, aromatic blend # 32 (tomato salad, p. 176) for basting flatbread and as a substitute for cold butter on boiled potatoes. And I use aromatic blend # 28 (silky fragrant leeks, p. 160) to boil salmon in. If I have some aromatic blend left over, even if it's only a few tablespoons, I save it and use it as a topping on soups and rice. Or, I add it to a pan of cabbage or spinach leaves. The point is that you should make the aromatic blends a part of your own cooking. Vary them and try them in new combinations. I encourage you to experiment.

VARY THE AROMATIC BLENDS AND TRY THEM IN NEW COMBINATIONS. I ENCOURAGE YOU TO EXPERIMENT

CAN THE AROMATIC BLENDS BE USED FOR BOTH FRYING AND BAKING?

Once you make an aromatic blend, you'll automatically want to use it for all kinds of other dishes. The majority of the aromatic blends are robust and stable enough to be used on the stove rather than in the oven as the recipe states. Thus, it's not inconceivable that aroma mixture # 4, which is used as a salad dressing (Crisp Salad of Bitter Endives p. 40), could also be used to pan-fry and caramelize carrots. Conversely, aroma mixture # 19, which is usually spread on chicken for roasting (baked flattened chicken, p. 118), could certainly be used to pan-fry small pieces of chicken, lamb, or fish.

WHY ARE TOPPINGS USED IN SOME OF THE RECIPES?

Adding a topping creates a more aesthetic effect, and often underlines a point. For example, in the recipe for glazed carrots (p. 68), I could have added the toppings (drained yogurt and fresh cilantro) directly to the pan, at the last minute, so the carrots sit in a creamy, sour sauce. But the point of the recipe is to illustrate how well loomi tastes on its own, and how it adds a unique shot of warming citrus, so it makes more sense to keep the toppings separate, even though both versions taste good.

WHY DO YOU STATE AMOUNTS FOR THE AROMATIC BLENDS?

Amounts are appropriate as soon as you start using aromatic blends with other ingredients, or when you use the aromatic blends in preparations other than those specified in the recipe. In a few instances, you'll use less than you've made. This is because once you start, it's hardly worthwhile to make a small amount of a specific aromatic blend. Most keep for a day or more, and will not go to waste. I have been consistent and specified quantities in all the aromatic blends. Sometimes, as mentioned, this may be relevant, while at other times it may seem superfluous.

HOW LONG WILL THE AROMATIC BLENDS KEEP?

It all depends on what they're made of and how they're prepared. An aromatic blend that consists entirely of ground, dried spices can last for several months. On the other hand, chopped fresh roots and herbs mixed with various liquids should often be used immediately. Other aromatic blends will benefit from standing for a few hours, or even a day or two, before being used. You will find this information at the end of the preparation description for each aromatic blend.

BEFORE YOU START—TOOLS, TIPS & EQUIPMENT

ABOUT THE RECIPES

I encourage you to follow my recipes to the letter, tempered with common sense. That way you'll be set up for success. I also want to emphasize that we can only be as good as the ingredients we buy. The quality of the ingredients is, and always will be, the most important element in creating an overall taste experience. In some recipes, such as in the crisp raw kohlrabi salad (p. 48), I specify precisely how an ingredient should be cut. I do so to make sure that you get exactly the aroma experience I intended. At other times, I specify an exact pan size. If, for example, you select a larger pan for the chard gratin (p. 52), it will affect the end result. The moisture from the ingredients will evaporate too quickly, and instead of putting your fork into a juicy, crispy gratin, you'll be left with a bland, bone-dry dish. In other recipes, I'm more relaxed, because a little less or a little more of something will not make much difference. The book includes only a few main dishes, but by simply toasting a piece of sourdough bread, boiling a potato, steaming some rice, or serving a green salad, most of the recipes can easily be turned into a main course. You can also do this by increasing the amounts, or by adding more ingredients in combination with the aromatic blend. And if you are baking, remember that I use a convection oven. If you use a regular (conventional) oven, you should increase the temperature by about 10°C (50°F).

BLACK PEPPER VS. CHILI FLAKES

Sometimes you've just had enough of something! And that's how I felt about black pepper, a spice that is always accompanied by salt, with both of them ground and added to a dish at start and finish. On the day that I overdid black pepper, and destroyed an entire meal, I asked myself: "Do I really need freshly ground black pepper with each and every dish, every single day?" It's an interesting question. Perhaps I could find something that would be better suited to the food I cook, but just as universal? Now it's been some years since I mostly gave up black pepper. Today I add a pinch or less of chili flakes instead. The flakes are used sparingly to give food a 'spark'. It is a kind of movement, or feeling, if you will. Chili flakes have a relatively neutral odor and taste, and a warm, uplifting effect that's not too strong. Having said that, there is a big difference in the strength and flavor of chili flakes. Get to know your chili flakes before using them as a kind of peppercorn. Or, try making your own: See 'How to maximize flavor' (p. 60).

SPEARMINT VS. PEPPERMINT

Fresh spearmint (*Mentha spicata*) is a favorite of mine and I use it frequently and very generously in my recipes. Spearmint has a warm, spicy, and sweet taste, with notes of cleansing light resin. It is universal yet distinctive. Peppermint varieties (*Mentha piperita*) I use only rarely. They demand a little more attention when adding to a dish, as they contain more of the dominant and cooling menthol aroma, and lack the delicate and soft sweetness of spearmint. If you're unsure whether you're holding a bunch of spearmint or peppermint, close your eyes, rub the leaves gently with your fingertips, and inhale. You will no longer be in doubt. There are hundreds of interesting spearmint varieties, such as spicy Moroccan mint (*Mentha spicata var. crispa*) or classic English green mint (*Mentha spicata v.*). But I must be careful with what I say about mint, as there are many with wonderfully beautiful aromas. All the varieties are worth trying, so you can find your own favorites.

TRUE CEYLON CINNAMON VS. CASSIA CINNAMON

I only use true Ceylon cinnamon (*Cinnamomum zeylanicum*) in my recipes. It is delicate and feminine, and not to be confused with the rock-hard and masculine cassia cinnamon (*Cinnamomum cassia*). They are like night and day, so it is essential to buy the right one. You can read more about Ceylon cinnamon and cassia cinnamon in 'The essentials of herbs and spices' (p. 274).

SEA SALT

I mostly use flaked sea salt. It has become both a routine and a ritual for me—I'm addicted to both the sound and the feeling

of quickly crushing the flakes between my fingers and adding them to dishes. Sea salt is indispensable in dressings and salads, and can be sprinkled over fried vegetables, meat, and fish. For dishes that require longer cooking, I use damp, gray sea salt that's unrefined and has no additives. You can use fine sea salt for quick meals, or grind coarse sea salt in a mortar. Remember that coarse sea salt needs at least six to ten minutes to dissolve, so take your time. There are big differences in the taste of various sea salts, but they all have fresh, pure notes that are never dull, neutral, or dominant.

OIL AND VINEGAR

Unfiltered apple cider vinegar is fresh and less sharp than other vinegars, and has subtle sweetness and fruitiness. If you need even more sweetness, choose a mature balsamic apple cider vinegar. Cold-pressed olive oil is another favorite, as it's filled with fresh and light fruity notes. It also has the ability to navigate my very generous use of spices, and helps balance the acidity in many of my dishes.

WHOLE SPICES VS. GROUND SPICES

Because they're intact, whole spices contain more aromatic compounds. As soon as spices are ground, their aromatic substances are reduced. This is inevitable, because the aromatic substances, the essential oils, are volatile, which means they quickly evaporate and change when exposed to oxygen, moisture, heat, or light. Just like coffee, spices are at their best when newly roasted, freshly ground, and used immediately. If a spice is difficult to grind or mill, add a pinch of sea salt or sugar, depending on what the spice is being used for, and, *voilà,* you have a uniform, white, powdered sugarlike spice mixture. If a recipe calls for a whole spice, you can use ground spice in the same amount—for the best results, use a scale rather than measuring spoons—but the flavor will be less expressive and convincing.

ROAST THE SPICES

Read more in 'How to maximize flavor' (p. 60).

SCALES AND MEASURING TOOLS

For accuracy and the best end results, I strongly recommend using a kitchen scale to measure ingredients. A digital scale is preferable, especially when measuring spices and herbs, where a few extra seeds or leaves can significantly affect the final taste of a dish. I have two scales. The smaller one can weigh amounts from 0.01 g (0.00035 oz) to 200 g (7 oz). I use this for measuring spices, because small seeds and leaves weigh less than 1 g (0.035 oz). The larger scale can weigh amounts from 1 g (0.035 oz) to 3 kg (6 ¾ lb). Alternatively, you can use measuring spoons, which are more accurate than measuring cups. Buy a set of six spoons, ranging from ⅛ tsp (0.6 ml) to 1 tbsp

(15 ml). It's also helpful to have a set of measuring cups with seven cups, ranging from 30 ml (2 tbsp) to 240 ml (1 cup). All the amounts used in the recipes are leveled at the top.

ELECTRIC COFFEE GRINDER VS. STONE MORTAR

Using an electric coffee grinder is a quick and efficient way to grind whole spices to a fine powder, especially if the amount is large and the mixture contains, for example, loomi (dried lime), which has a relatively tough texture. I have two electric coffee grinders. One I use for sweet spices like cardamom, cinnamon, cloves, allspice, and the like; the other I use for powerful, fragrant spices, such as cumin and fenugreek. A coffee grinder should be cleaned three or four times a year, by grinding a few spoonfuls of sugar to a fine powder (discard the ground sugar) and then drying it thoroughly with a cloth. A stone mortar is handy if you're only grinding a few tablespoons or less, as a coffee grinder simply can't blend small quantities of spices evenly. In a stone mortar, you have more control over how finely or coarsely the spices are ground. The mortar is also great for all kinds of wet mashing, and can be used with fresh spices such as chili, garlic, lemon grass, ginger, and turmeric, as well as herbs. The herbs and spices don't lose any moisture or leave their aroma on the cutting board, so the results are juicy and full of flavor. You might be tempted to use a food processor, but the results won't be the same.

MANDOLINE SLICER

If you like uniform, paper-thin slices of fruits and vegetables, get an Asian-style mandoline slicer. It makes the cutting process much easier, and provides a quick and easy way to add textural variety to various foods. Buy one made of plastic, as they are cheaper and easier to use than the expensive and heavy versions made of stainless steel.

RASP GRATER

A rasp grater is a fantastic little lightweight tool that can add a touch of aroma to any dish in a split second and with very little effort. It's absolutely indispensable when cooking with bitter almonds, citrus zest, or fresh turmeric and ginger. Invest in two rasp graters: one fine and one medium.

MODERN PRESSURE COOKER

Using a pressure cooker saves time and preserves valuable aromas. The food, because it is tightly sealed in, retains more aromatic compounds and nutrients than if you use a regular pot with a lid. A pressure cooker is particularly suitable for cheaper cuts of meat and bean dishes that require prolonged cooking to become tender. The rule of thumb, when using a pressure cooker, is to divide the normal cooking time by three, but always read the manufacturer's instructions for guidance. Remember to let the dish stand for at least thirty minutes, so the juices can redistribute and the muscles can relax. Resting food cooked in a pressure cooker is also essential to its taste, so be patient.

OLD-FASHIONED CAST IRON FRYING PAN

Cast iron pots and pans have been used for hundreds of years, and are beautiful, timeless pieces that never wear out. The material is fantastic, because the heat is distributed evenly and uniformly, while the thick base prevents food from burning. I use my (25 cm / 10 in diameter) cast iron frying pan every day, either on the induction stove, the gas stove, the outdoor grill, or in the oven. It's perfect for omelets, pancakes, meat, vegetables, breads, pies, and cakes.

SALAD SPINNER

Very wet salads, herbs, and cabbage leaves can be spun in a salad spinner to ensure they're dry and delicious. If the leaves are not completely dry when chopped, their aromatic substances will mix with the residual water, and go to waste on the cutting board. When making salads, it is a great advantage for the leaves to be completely dry, as the dressing will stick to the leaves, rather than fall to the bottom of the salad bowl.

MIXING BOWL

Choose a mixing bowl made of porcelain, earthenware, glazed stoneware, tempered glass, or stainless steel, all of which will eventually acquire a beautiful patina. In other words, buy a bowl you are going to keep and not throw out. In my view, mixing bowls can never be too big. Although I only cook for two people, I always use my largest bowl, so there's room for big arm movements when mixing, stirring, and kneading away. There is nothing worse than not having enough room, and having to be careful—then the food takes much longer to make. I prefer big, wide bowls rather than deep, narrow ones. The bowls should be able to accommodate a minimum of 3 to 4 l (12 to 16 cups) and have a diameter of at least 32 cm (12 in). Then you just need a dozen smaller bowls, preferably stackable, for this and that, and you're ready to go.

FOOD PROCESSOR

A food processor is an extra hand in the kitchen, when the chopping gets to be too much, or when mixtures need a smooth, glossy texture that your hand and a sharp knife cannot accomplish on their own. I use my food processor only a few times a month, but then it makes a big difference, and eases my work.

DEEP-FRYING IN A WOK

A wok is ideal for deep-frying, because it is lightweight and broad, with rounded edges. It also requires less oil, and provides better control when deep-frying. In the old days, woks were made of cast iron, but today aluminum is often used, which is less expensive and not as durable. My wok is made of thin cast iron, and was manufactured in Japan. It is relatively small (24 cm / 9½ in diameter) and despite being used regularly for the past fourteen years, it hasn't worn out. Cast iron woks can be found on the Internet. Successful deep-frying depends on a lot of things, but your worst enemy is moisture. The more moisture that arises during frying, the softer and less crisp the final result. With this in mind, avoid adding large amounts of ingredients, which will lower the oil temperature, and create moisture. Instead, deep-fry small amounts, giving the ingredients ample space. Make sure the oil is kept at the same temperature throughout the frying process and be sure to toss and turn the ingredients a few times while frying. The result will be uniformly golden, crispy ingredients that are cooked but still juicy inside.

JUST LIKE COFFEE, SPICES ARE AT THEIR BEST WHEN NEWLY ROASTED, FRESHLY GROUND, AND USED IMMEDIATELY

Choosing the right oil for deep-frying is at least as important as the ingredients. I don't use refined oils in my cooking. Expect to use around 1.5 l (6 cups), and invest in neutral, cold-pressed oils, such canola, peanut, or olive oil. Deep-frying typically takes place at around 150 to 190°C (300 to 375°F). If the oil starts to smoke, you've burned it, so take it off the heat immediately, and start over, as this will likely leave an unpleasant taste in the oil. If the oil temperature is kept under 200°C (395°F), it can be reused several times. Cool the oil slightly then pour it through a coffee filter or a fine sieve. Keep the oil in a clean jar, cool and dry, until the next time you need it. If you fry fish in the oil, it can only be used again with fish.

AROMATIC BLEND

KEY INGREDIENT	#1	#2	#3	#4	#5	#6	#7	#8	#9	#10	#11	#12	#13	#14	#15	#16	#17	#18	#19	#20	#21	#22
APPLE		○		○		○					○	○	○									
ASPARAGUS	○	○	○	○		○	○	○	○		○	○	○	○				○				
BEAN	○	○		○	○	○	○	○	○	○	○	○	○	○			○	○	○			
BEEF	○	○	○	○							○	○	○			○	○	○	○	○	○	○
BLACK CURRANT																						
BOK CHOY	○	○	36	○	○	○	○	○	○	○	○	○	○		○		○	○				
BRUSSELS SPROUT	28	○	○	○	○	○	○	○		○	○	○	○	○								
CARROT		○	○	○	○	○	○	○	68			○	○						○			
CAULIFLOWER	○	32	○	○			○	○	○			○	○					○	○			
CELERIAC	○	○					○			72		○	○					○	○			
CHARD	○						52															
CHICKEN	○	○	○	○	○	○	○	○	○		○	○	○	○	○	○	○	○	118	○	○	○
CHICKPEA	○				○	○				○					○			○				
CUCUMBER		○	○	○	○	○		○	○				○									
DRIED FRUIT																						
DUCK	○	○	○	○	○	○			○			○	○					○		122	○	○
EGG		○											○									
ENDIVE	○	○	○	40	○	○	○					○	○		○		○		○			
FENNEL	○	○		○	○	○					○	○	○					○	○			
FLOUR																						
GOOSEBERRY																						
KALE	○	○		○	44		○					○	○						○			
KOHLRABI		○	○			48	○					○	○									
LAMB	○	○	○	○	○	○	○	○	○	○	○	○	○	○	○	○	○	○	○	○	126	○
LEEK	○	○	○	○	○	○	○	○	○	○	○	○	○					○	○			
LENTIL		○			○							○	○				○					
MACKEREL	○	○	○	○	○	○	○	○	○	○	○	○	○	90	○	○	○	○	○	○	○	
MELON				○																		
MUSSEL	○	○						○				○	○	○	94		○	○				
ONION					○	○		○		○		○	○					○	○			
PEACH					○	○																
PEAR					○	○							○									
PORK	○	○	○	○	○				○	○		○	○	○	○	○	○	○	○	○	○	130
POTATO		○	○			○	○		○		76	○	○				○	○				
PUMPKIN		○				○	○		○			80	○				○		○			
QUINCE												○							○			
RADISH		○				○						○	○									
RASPBERRY																						
RHUBARB					○																	
RICE	○	○	○	○	○																	
SALMON	○	○	○	○	○	○	○	○	○	○	○	○	○	○	○	98	○	○	○	○		
SALSIFY	○	○				○	○		○		○	84										
SEED																						
SHRIMP	○	○	○			○	○	○	○				○	○	○		102	○	○			
SPINACH	○		○	○	○	○	○	56	○		○	○	○					○	○			
SQUID	○	○						○	○					○	○		○	106				
STRAWBERRY					○																	
TOMATO		○										○	○									
YOGURT		○																				
ZUCCHINI		○	○			○	○		○			○	○	○				○	○			

APPLICATION CHART FOR THE AROMATIC BLENDS

# 23	# 24	# 25	# 26	# 27	# 28	# 29	# 30	# 31	# 32	# 33	# 34	# 35	# 36	# 37	# 38	# 39	# 40	# 41	# 42	# 43	# 44	# 45	# 46	# 47	# 48	# 49	# 50
			O			O	O	O	O							O		**226**	O	O					O	O	O
	144	O	O	O	O	O	O	O																			
	O	**148**		O			O	O	O	O	O	O		O						O							
134	O	O	O			O	O				O			O							O						
																								O	O		**268**
	O	O	O	O	O	O	O	O	O		O	O		O							O						
	O	O	O	O	O	O	O	O	O		O	O		O													
	O	O	O	O	O	O	O	O	O		O						O			O	O	O					
	O	O	O	O	O	O	O	O	O		O			O							O						
	O	O	O				O															O					
	O	O	O		O		O																				
O	O	O	O			O		O	O		O		O														
	O	O	O					O		O	O	**186**	O	O													
	O	O	**152**					O	O	O										O							
														206		O		O									
O	O	O	O		O	O	O		O					O													O
	O	O					O				**190**																
	O	O	O				O				O			O													
	O	O	O	**156**		O	O	O														O					
											194																
																								256	O		O
	O	O		O			O		O		O																
	O		O				O											O									
O	O	O	O			O	O		O		O			O							O						
	O	O	**160**	O		O	O	O	O																		
	O	O	O			O	O		O	O	O		**198**	O													
	O	O				O			O		O										O						
		O				O	O			O	O										**234**		O	O	O		
						O	O		O	O	O																
	O	O		O		**164**	O				O																
	O	O	O			O		O	O	O						O			**230**				O	O	O	O	
		O	O			O				O						O			O	O	**238**					O	
O	O					O					O			O													
	O	O		O	O		O		O								O				O						
	O	O					O	O	O		O	O										O					
								O													O	**242**				O	
	O	O	O			O		**172**								O							O	O	**260**	O	O
																							246	O	O	O
								O	O	O		**202**													O	
O	O	O		O		O	O	O	O	O	O		O													
O	O			O			O														O					
													214													
O	O	O				O			O		O															
O	O					O			O		O										O					
								O																			
																O		O				O	O	O	**264**
	O	O			O	O	O	**176**			O					O									O	
	O						O			O					**210**						O	O			O
		O		O	O	O	**168**		O																	

Please adjust the recipe accordingly if using a different key ingredient than in the original.

● = PAGE NUMBER OF ORIGINAL RECIPE

CRUNCHY LEAVES AND CABBAGES

SPEARMINT/TURMERIC ROOT/NIGELLA/LEMON/ PALM SUGAR/CORIANDER SEED/CHILI/RED ONION/ APPLE/YOGURT/GINGER ROOT/GARLIC/CUMIN

BRUSSELS SPROUT

WARM BRUSSELS SPROUT SALAD

500 g (18 oz) cleaned Brussels sprouts

CHARACTER

A highly aromatic, piquant, and tart blend with a juicy, creamy texture.

VARIATIONS

The aromatic blend can also be used as a base for chicken and potato salads, or used with fish and shellfish. Fold it with warm pasta or steaming hot bok choy cabbage. Use cold, as a spread on flatbread, or in sandwiches, perhaps with slices of smoked mackerel and salmon.

AROMATIC BLEND #1

2 g (1 tsp) whole cumin seeds
2 g (1 tsp) whole coriander seeds
1 g (½ tsp) whole nigella seeds
45 ml (3 tbsp) cold-pressed olive oil, for frying
50 g (3½ tbsp) finely chopped red onion
15 g (1 tbsp) finely chopped fresh ginger with peel
2 (10 g) cloves garlic, finely chopped
4 g (½ tbsp) finely chopped fresh turmeric with peel
A pinch of chili flakes
45 ml (3 tbsp) freshly squeezed lemon juice
45 ml (3 tbsp) boiling water
10 g (2 tsp) coarsely grated palm sugar, or light cane sugar
Sea salt
70 g (2 ½ oz) drained yogurt (min. 10% fat)
60 g (2 oz) diced cooking apple with peel
5 g (1 tbsp) finely chopped fresh spearmint

This is an ultra-creamy, full-bodied, and highly aromatic salad. It's no secret that I'm addicted to and a big fan of tartness in food, whether it comes from hibiscus flowers, sumac, vinegar, tamarind paste, loomi, citrus fruits, pomegranate, or other fresh fruit and unfiltered fruit juices. They all give food an edge, and make it more interesting. As the tartness purifies, it gives your tongue peace and calm. And this aromatic blend is no exception. When making the blend, be sure to cook the red onion until golden brown and caramelized; otherwise, the dish will lack its essential nuttiness.

AROMATIC BLEND

Put the cumin, coriander, and nigella seeds in an electric coffee grinder or mortar and pestle and grind to a fine powder. Heat a saucepan over high heat and add the cold-pressed olive oil. Add the freshly ground spices, along with the red onion, ginger, garlic, turmeric, and chili flakes. Sauté for 3–5 minutes, or until the red onion turns golden brown. Take the pan off the heat, add the lemon juice, boiling water, and palm sugar, and season with sea salt. Add the yogurt, apple, and spearmint, fold the mixture together, and keep warm. Durability: Serve immediately, while still warm. Makes 300 ml (1 ¼ cups).

BRUSSELS SPROUTS

Trim the roots off the Brussels sprouts and remove any discolored leaves. Wash the Brussels sprouts and divide them carefully into leaves with a small, sharp knife, or cut them into very thin slices. Put the Brussels sprout leaves in a large bowl and add just enough boiling water to cover. Let stand for 5 minutes then strain. Fold in the warm aromatic blend and serve immediately.

SEASON: November–March
Starter or side dish for 4

SEA SALT FLAKES / OLIVE OIL / CORIANDER SEED / GARLIC

CAULIFLOWER

ROASTED CAULIFLOWER

2 heads cauliflower (1.5 kg / 3 ⅓ lb)

CHARACTER
A rich, crunchy, and tangy blend with a subtle nutty attitude and slight bitterness; very addictive.

VARIATIONS
The aromatic blend can also be used with leeks, broccoli, potatoes, cabbage, asparagus, root vegetables, seafood, and steak. Always add the topping last.

AROMATIC BLEND #2
12 (60 g) cloves garlic
10 g (2 tbsp) whole coriander seeds
45 ml (3 tbsp) cold-pressed olive oil, for frying
Sea salt flakes

45 ml (3 tbsp) Worcestershire sauce (topping)
75 g (5 tbsp) freshly shaved Parmesan (topping)

Masculine and full-bodied, this is a juicy and crunchy vegetable dish. The coriander and garlic must be cooked until golden brown and crisp, or the aromatic blend will taste much too bitter, so pay careful attention to the 2 to 3 minutes required. You'll be rewarded with a blend that's ultra-crisp and very delicate, with piquant nutty notes. If there are leftovers, the cauliflower is delicious in sandwiches, as a topping for cold cuts on rye bread, or in green salads.

AROMATIC BLEND
Crush the garlic with the lower part of your palm or a mortar and pestle to loosen the skins. Peel the garlic then mash it coarsely with the mortar and pestle and put it in a small bowl. Put the coriander seeds in an electric coffee grinder or a mortar and pestle and grind to a coarse powder. Add the powder to the mashed garlic and mix to combine.

Heat a medium frying pan over medium-high heat and add the cold-pressed olive oil. Sauté the garlic and coriander mixture, stirring frequently to prevent burning, for 2–3 minutes, or until crunchy and golden brown; season with sea salt flakes. Set aside. Durability: 2 days at room temperature. Makes 180 ml (¾ cup).

CAULIFLOWER
Remove any light green leaves and the coarse stem at the base of the cauliflower then divide it into small florets (the cleaned weight should be approx. 1 kg / 2 ¼ lb). Put the cauliflower in a parchment paper–lined roasting pan. Bake in a preheated 230°C (450°F) oven for 30–45 minutes, or until dark brown. As soon as the cauliflower comes out of the oven, drizzle it with the Worcestershire sauce, so the florets can absorb as much flavor as possible. Let stand for a few minutes then serve, topped with the aromatic blend and shaved Parmesan.

SEASON: July–October
Starter or side dish for 4–6

LEMON / SEA SALT / CHILI FLAKES / CANE SUGAR / ELDERFLOWER / RADISH / APPLE CIDER VINEGAR

BOK CHOY

SWEET AND SOUR SAUTÉED BOK CHOY

400 g (14 oz) bok choy

CHARACTER

A refined, sweet, sour, rich, warm, summery blend with light floral attitude and citrus notes.

VARIATIONS

The aromatic blend can also be used with boiled and fried vegetables, such as cabbage, beets, new onions, rhubarb, and potatoes, or as a marinade for thinly sliced vegetables.

AROMATIC BLEND #3

75 ml (⅓ cup) unfiltered apple cider vinegar
60 ml (4 tbsp) water
50 g (3½ tbsp) light cane sugar
20 g (4 tsp) elderflower umbels without stalks
10 g (2 tbsp) finely grated lemon zest
4 g (½ tsp) sea salt
0.5 g (¼ tsp) chili flakes
200 g (7 oz) paper-thin slices radish
30 ml (2 tbsp) freshly squeezed lemon juice

Cold-pressed olive oil, for frying

Bok choy (small) and pak choy (large) are varieties of Chinese cabbage. With just a few minutes over high heat, they deliver fantastic juiciness, fine sweetness, light cabbage notes, and a crunchy texture. I make this aromatic blend every year, as soon as the elderflower umbels in the garden open up, and herald the arrival of summer. Don't wash the elderflowers, as that will remove the honey sweetness of their pollen. Instead, shake them, so that any insects fall off or run away—and do this outside! The elderflower umbels can be replaced by fresh mint, dill, or tarragon, or the flowers of chives, thyme, or arugula. If there are any leftovers, try leaving the sautéed cabbage in the aromatic blend overnight (there is plenty of liquid) and you will get a lightly pickled vegetable instead.

AROMATIC BLEND

Put the apple cider vinegar, water, light cane sugar, elderflower umbels, lemon zest, sea salt, and chili flakes in a small saucepan and cover. Bring to a boil over high heat and cook for 2 minutes then turn off the heat. Take out the elderflower umbels, using a fork, then chop them finely. Put the umbels back in the saucepan, along with the radishes and lemon juice, and let stand for 15 minutes before using. Keep warm. Durability: 1–2 weeks refrigerated. Makes 400 ml (1 ⅔ cup).

BOK CHOY

Trim the roots off the bok choy, leaving them intact as much as possible, then cut in half lengthwise. Heat a medium frying pan/wok over high heat and add a little cold-pressed olive oil. Sauté the cabbages over high heat for 2–3 minutes per side, or until tender but still crisp. Put the bok choy in a large bowl, add the warm aromatic blend, and toss to coat.

SEASON: July–October
Starter or side dish for 4–6

SEA SALT / SAFFRON / APPLE JUICE / OLIVE OIL / DATES

ENDIVE

CRISP SALAD OF BITTER ENDIVES

300 g (10 ½ oz) whole endive and/or radicchio

CHARACTER
A warm and creamy blend that's sweet, tangy, and exotic.

VARIATIONS
The aromatic blend can also be used with ripe fruit, such as melon, on all sorts of salads, or as a dip for warm flatbread.

AROMATIC BLEND #4
2 (20 g) fresh Medjool dates
200 ml (13 tbsp) unfiltered apple juice
A pinch of saffron
30 ml (2 tbsp) cold-pressed olive oil
Sea salt

130 g (4 ½ oz) unpeeled, cored, and thinly sliced apple
5 g (1 tbsp) finely grated fresh horseradish (topping)

This is a highly aromatic, tangy, sweet, and slightly bitter winter salad. Make the aromatic blend at the last minute, so it's still hot when you toss it with the crisp lettuce leaves. Orange segments or sliced pear can be substituted for the apple, if desired. The fresh horseradish topping is particularly interesting. It turns the whole taste experience upside down and is a must.

AROMATIC BLEND
Remove the seeds from the dates. Put the dates in a small saucepan, along with the apple juice and saffron, and bring to a boil over high heat. Boil for 5 minutes, or until the liquid is reduced to 100 ml (7 tbsp). Turn off the heat, add the cold-pressed olive oil, and season with sea salt. Durability: Use immediately. Makes 130 ml (9 tbsp).

ENDIVE
Cut the ends off the endive and divide the heads into leaves or cut the heads cross-wise into strips. Put the endive in a large bowl, add the sliced apples and the warm aromatic blend, and toss to combine. Top with the horseradish, and serve immediately.

SEASON: November–March
Starter or side dish for 4

WATER / GINGER ROOT / BLACK CARDAMOM / PISTACHIOS / CREAMED COCONUT

KALE

CREAMY AND CRUNCHY KALE

350 g (12 ¼ oz) cavolo nero or curly kale

CHARACTER

A creamy, sweet, and exotic blend domi-nated by fresh tangy ginger, warm coconut, and elegant smokiness.

VARIATIONS

The aromatic blend can also be used with seafood, cabbages, or spinach, as well as beans and other legumes, and boiled grains, such as rice, couscous, and bulgur.

AROMATIC BLEND #5

4 (4 g) black cardamom pods (see p. 277)
100 g (3 ½ oz) coarsely chopped creamed coconut
30 g (2 tbsp) finely chopped fresh ginger with peel
20 g (2 tbsp) coarsely chopped pistachios
150 ml (10 tbsp) boiling water

Cold-pressed olive oil, for frying
Sea salt
30 g (1 oz) dried apple slices (topping)

Everything about this dish is easy. Get hold of some large dried apple slices—not small cubes. This will give you lots of dominant fruity sweetness with each bite, which is essential. Almonds can be substituted for the pistachios. The aromatic blend isn't boiled, so it's important to let it stand for the full 15 to 30 minutes to enhance the smoky flavor notes from the black carda-mom.

AROMATIC BLEND

Crush the cardamom pods with something heavy, such as a pestle, so they will be easier to open. Remove the seeds (discard the pods), put them in an electric coffee grinder or mortar and pestle, and grind to a fine powder. Put the powder in a medium bowl, add the creamed coconut, ginger, pistachios, and boiling water and let stand for 15–30 minutes. If the aromatic blend is too thick, add a little extra boiling water. Keep warm. Durability: Use immediately. Makes 240 ml (1 cup).

KALE

Pull the kale leaves off the stems then rinse and dry them (the cleaned weight should be approx. 280 g / 10 oz); discard the stems. Heat a large frying pan over high heat and add a little cold-pressed olive oil. Sauté the kale—work in 2 batches, if nec-essary—over high heat for 8–10 minutes, or until curled up and tender. Season with sea salt, turn off the heat, and toss with the warm aromatic blend. Top with the dried apple slices and serve immediately.

SEASON: September–February
Starter or side dish for 4

OLIVE OIL / MUSCOVADO CANE SUGAR / SEA SALT / GINGER ROOT / BLOOD ORANGE JUICE / FENNEL SEED / TARRAGON

KOHLRABI

CRISP RAW KOHLRABI SALAD

2 large kohlrabies (600 g / 21 oz)

CHARACTER

An aromatic blend with quiet tanginess and notes of elegant anise and warm caramel.

VARIATIONS

The aromatic blend can also be used with a salad of bitter greens and feta, as a cold sauce for fried fish, or tossed with finely chopped vegetables to make coleslaw.

AROMATIC BLEND #6

45 ml (3 tbsp) freshly squeezed blood orange juice
30 ml (2 tbsp) cold-pressed olive oil
15 g (1 tbsp) finely chopped fresh ginger with peel
10 g (1 tbsp) dark muscovado cane sugar
5 g (1 tbsp) finely chopped fresh tarragon
0.5 g (⅛ tsp) whole fennel seeds
Sea salt

Refreshing and crunchy, this salad is easy to make and completely addictive. Cut the kohlrabi into large cubes to ensure you get plenty of the vegetable's juicy sweetness in elegant combination with the tangy aromatic blend.

AROMATIC BLEND

Put the blood orange juice, cold-pressed olive oil, ginger, dark muscovado cane sugar, and tarragon in a small bowl. Put the fennel seeds in a mortar and pestle and grind to a fine powder. Add the powder to the aromatic blend and season with sea salt. Durability: Use the same day. Makes 120 ml (½ cup).

KOHLRABI

If you buy kohlrabi in the winter, the skin is often very thick and woody. If that's the case, trim the tops and bottoms then peel the skin with a sharp knife to reveal the juicy, glassy flesh (the peeled weight should be approx. 400 g / 14 oz). Very young kohlrabi, harvested in late summer, can easily be peeled with a potato peeler. Cut the kohlrabi into large, uniform cubes (approx. 1.5 cm / ⅝ in) and put in a large bowl. Add the aromatic blend, toss to coat, and serve immediately.

SEASON: June–January
Starter or side dish for 4

FENNEL SEED / CEYLON CINNAMON / CREAM / BLACK PEPPERCORN / JUNIPER / BREAD / CARDAMOM / FETA / PAPRIKA / BACON

CHARD

CHARD GRATIN

500 g (18 oz) chard

CHARACTER
A full-bodied, juicy, and warm blend that's very aromatic.

VARIATIONS
The aromatic blend can also be used with watery vegetables and cabbage varieties, such as fennel, squash, Chinese cabbage, pointed cabbage, cauliflower, Brussels sprouts, broccoli, and bok choy.

AROMATIC BLEND #7
2.5 cm (1 in) (2 g) Ceylon cinnamon stick
10 (1 g) whole juniper berries
1 g (½ tsp) whole fennel seeds
10 (0.6 g) whole black peppercorns
3 (0.75 g) cardamom pods
150 ml (10 tbsp) heavy cream
4 g (2 tsp) sweet paprika
100 g (3 ½ oz) day-old bread without crust, cut into chunks
150 g (5 ¼ oz) coarsely crumbled feta
100 g (3 ½ oz) whole bacon slices

Cold-pressed olive oil, for baking

Simple and rustic, this makes for a very tasty everyday meal. Add the feta, bread, and chard in relatively large pieces, so they'll hold plenty of moisture, even after they've been baked crisp. Resist the temptation to add salt, even when you're boiling the chard. There is plenty of salt in both the feta and the bacon though the bacon is not absolutely necessary for this dish to hit the mark.

AROMATIC BLEND
Put the cinnamon, juniper berries, fennel seeds, peppercorns, and cardamom pods in an electric coffee grinder or mortar and pestle and grind to a fine powder. Put the powder in a small bowl, add the cream and paprika, and whisk to combine. Durability: Use immediately. Makes 180 ml (¾ cup).

CHARD
Divide the chard into tops (the green leaves) and stems (the white parts), and remove some of the coarse root. Cut the leaves into 3 cm (1 ¼ in) wide strips and cut the stems into 2 cm (¾ in) long pieces. In a pot of boiling water, cook the stems for 3–4 minutes. Add the leaves and boil for 1 more minute. Immediately drain the chard in a colander and let cool.

When the chard leaves and stems are cool enough to handle, squeeze them hard to remove any excess water.

Fold the chard leaves and stems and the chunks of bread into the aromatic blend then spread the mixture in a greased ovenproof round casserole/baking dish (about 25 cm/10 in diameter). Sprinkle the feta and the raw bacon slices on top, drizzle with a little cold-pressed olive oil, and bake in a preheated 200°C (395°F) oven for 30 minutes, or until golden brown on top. Serve immediately.

SEASON: May–September
Starter or side dish for 4

WATER / CHILI / NUOC MAM /
LIME JUICE / FENNEL / PALM
SUGAR / GARLIC / CILANTRO

SPINACH

QUICK SAUTÉED SPINACH

350 g (12 ¼ oz) cleaned spinach with stems

CHARACTER

A sweet, sour, and tangy blend dominated by Asian fish sauce, with subtle anise notes and a juicy, crunchy texture.

VARIATIONS

The aromatic blend can also be used with other vegetables, including cabbages and root vegetables, with fish or seafood, or on top of boiled rice, grains, and pulses.

AROMATIC BLEND #8

15 g (3 tsp) coarsely grated palm sugar, or light cane sugar
15 ml (1 tbsp) boiling water
30 ml (2 tbsp) nuoc mam / nam pla (fish sauce)
30 ml (2 tbsp) freshly squeezed lime juice
75 g (6 tbsp) finely chopped fennel bulb
15 g (3 tbsp) fresh cilantro with stems, coarsely chopped
2 (10 g) cloves garlic, finely chopped
10 g (1 tbsp) finely chopped fresh green chili with seeds

75 g (6 tbsp) finely chopped, blanched, roasted, unsalted peanuts (topping)

This dish is filling, juicy, and not too strongly flavored. Use spinach leaves with stems, ideally thick juicy stems that will stay crunchy and moist after cooking. Make this dish quickly and over high heat. There's no need for added salt, as the nuoc mam / nam pla, or fish sauce (an extract of small fermented fish and salt), has plenty of salinity.

AROMATIC BLEND

In a small bowl, combine the palm sugar and boiling water and whisk to dissolve the sugar. Add the nuoc mam / nam pla, lime juice, fennel, cilantro, garlic, and green chili. Durability: Use the same day. Makes 200 ml (13 tbsp).

SPINACH

Heat a large frying pan over high heat. Add the aromatic blend and let it sputter and bubble slightly for a few seconds; do not turn down the heat. Add the spinach and sauté less than 1 minute, or until the spinach wilts and the liquid is significantly reduced. Serve the spinach piping hot, topped with peanuts.

SEASON: May–October
Starter or side dish for 4

HOW TO MAXIMIZE FLAVOR

When you mix two or more spices together, a fascinating chemical reaction takes place that can best be described as a cross between a fistfight and a ballet. And when you cook with spices, it completely changes the rules of the game, because the aromatic compounds, the essential oils, are affected and altered by each other. Just like we human beings, spices are influenced by the presence of other spices. Some that usually dominate become milder, while others step into character and overtake completely, and others surprise us with new,

ROASTING AND GRINDING SPICES YOURSELF CAN BE AN ALMOST MEDITATIVE EXPERIENCE

interesting potential, depending on how they're combined. It all depends on the interactions of ingredients, as well as the quantity, size, cooking time, and temperature. This intermezzo can last minutes, hours, days, weeks, or even months. It's why a soup or stew can have a more expressive taste the day after it's made and why a salad dressing can be altered significantly if it is simply allowed to stand for an extra half an hour. Conversely, a few minutes can be enough time for something extraordinary to happen, as in a good cup of coffee or tea. In sum, even when the bread is baked, the meat grilled,

the vegetables fried, and the juices boiled, their aromatic substances will change over time, albeit more slowly and less dramatically. Sometimes you can figure it all out, other times you can't. But it's rarely boring.

THE ART OF RETAINING AN AROMA
Spices possess hundreds of invisible aromas—their essential oils—that are concentrated and highly volatile, which means they're light enough and small enough to slip up our noses and into our mouths as we breathe. When spices are ground, or exposed to high temperatures, the aromatic compounds become even more volatile. And that opens up a whole new luxurious universe. Without sophisticated distillation apparatus, it's quite impossible to catch all the aromatic substances, so the art is finding a way to capture most of them for as long as possible. Most of the aromatic substances are fat-soluble, and can therefore be mixed with fats, such as butter and oil. The fat can come from all sorts of ingredients. Animal and plant-based fats are particularly effective, but vinegar, alcohol, and sugar contain microscopic fat molecules and can be useful in the struggle to pin down aromatic substances. If you sauté freshly ground spices in fat for a few minutes, your dish will end up with a much better taste and scent.

ROAST THE SPICES
It takes less than fifteen seconds to get even more flavor from whole spices. A short dry-roasting at a high temperature intensifies aromas and magnifies flavor, so that a spice's personality shines through more clearly. It creates a greater and broader aroma profile, even though the overall expression is milder and more harmonious. Roasting also turns spices brittle, which makes them easier to grind in a mortar. And roasting and grinding spices yourself can be an almost meditative experience. Here's how to do it: Heat a small frying pan over high heat then add the whole spices. Dry-roast the spices until they smell lovely and begin to take on a little color. If the pan is good and hot, this takes no more than five to fifteen seconds. Immediately pour the spices onto a plate to prevent burning

then put them in an electric coffee grinder or a mortar, and grind them to a fine powder. Use the powder immediately, or store it in a tightly sealed container; otherwise, the volatile aromas will evaporate and go to waste.

JUST LIKE WE HUMAN BEINGS, SPICES ARE INFLUENCED BY OTHER SPICES

GRIND YOUR OWN SPICES

The degree to which whole spices are ground can have a profound effect on their taste. In combination with the proper cooking time and temperature, you can more or less control how much flavor you'll release by selecting just the right amount of grinding. A whole seed lies in a kind of hibernation state, and gives off very few aromas. When you grind a spice, you make its surface area larger, so the aromatic substances wake up, and can quickly enter a dish. If you use whole spices, they require a minimum of one hour of cooking, preferably longer, if they are to fully contribute to a dish. Coarsely ground spices require much less time, while a finely ground powder can provide aromatic intensity in just five to fifteen minutes. Most people buy spices in powdered form, but it's important to remember that if you subject powdered spice to several hours of cooking, it will lose much of its aroma. In that case, I recommend seasoning before, during, and at the end of cooking to maximize the aromas.

GRAY MUSTARD SEEDS

Brown and black mustard seeds are brilliant condiments, because they're crunchy and taste beautifully of nuts, but are much less expensive. In order to release their attractive nutty aromas, these strong, bitter seeds first need to be roasted. What to do: Heat a small frying pan over high heat then add the mustard seeds and dry-roast them for ten to fifteen seconds, or until they begin to 'jump' and change color to gray. This technique mellows the mustard seeds, breaking down their enzymes and amplifying their nutty aromas and sweetness, while also diminishing almost all trace of bitterness. Another good option is to sauté mustard seeds in fat until they turn gray

in color. Whether cooked with or without oil, roasted mustard seeds can be added, while they're still sizzling hot, to soups, hot sauces, dips, and fruit chutneys, where they'll add a tremendous boost of flavor.

USING FRESH GINGER

Fresh ginger is something quite special: It is undoubtedly a favorite ingredient, and is therefore included in most of my recipes. It can act like chilis, delivering a searing and uplifting feeling to a dish that cleanses the palate, and makes room for other ingredients. This sensory effect is due to the fact that ginger contains gingerol, an aromatic substance that's affected by cooking time and temperature. If ginger is exposed to high heat for a few minutes, or prepared as a tea, its lively and elegant top notes of citrus and eucalyptus come forward, while prolonged boiling or baking reduces its strength—the top notes disappear—and produces more sweetness and a deeper flavor. On the other hand, drying ginger—that is, using ginger powder—dramatically reduces its attractive top notes, while making the root almost twice as strong. As with spices, you can adjust the aromatic intensity of ginger root (and turmeric root) by cutting it a particular way, and adjusting the cooking time and temperature. If you finely grate ginger, you'll immediately experience a lively and vigorous rush of aroma, but if the root is chopped, it will be much milder. I use finely grated ginger if the cooking time is less than ten to fifteen minutes, and add fine, medium, and coarsely chopped ginger to dishes that cook for more than fifteen minutes. You can also choose to season a dish at the very end to maintain the aromas.

TIME IS A SPICE

Time is a thief, but it is also an important tool in the kitchen. It demands no manual skill, but challenges your patience and your ability to plan. If, for example, we compare lightning-fast pan-fried shrimp salad (p. 102) to gravlax (p. 98), which takes several days, they each naturally have their own aromatic expressions, especially due to the different ingredients used. But it will always be time that creates the biggest difference. Time has the ability to mature the expression of ingredients, and create peace, balance, and harmony, especially if we turn our attention to texture, which is where time is the ultimate tool. On the other hand, ingredients cooked for just a few minutes over high heat, such as in a wok, can possess equally amazing textures. This is practiced most compellingly in street food, where dishes are typically super crunchy, cheeky, and intense. It's a dream cuisine in my view.

FRESH HERBS—EAU DE COLOGNE

Seventeen years ago, on the streets of Hanoi, I first tasted Phở, the traditional Vietnamese noodle soup. It was a revelation. I remember less about what was in the bottom of the bowl, and more about what lay on top—a tangle of green herbs that left me completely intoxicated. Exposed only to steam from the boiling hot soup, the finest top notes of Mexican coriander (*Eryngium foetidum*), Thai basil, Vietnamese Balm (*Elsholtzia ciliata*), cilantro, spearmint, peppermint, and Vietnamese coriander (*Polygonum odoratum*) were a gift to the senses. That's why, today, I use fresh herbs as a kind of citrus-based fragrance, and always add them at the very end of cooking. Summer flatbread chapatis (p. 194) are a good example of how just a few minutes at high heat can make more delicate flavors wide awake, full of charm, and present throughout a dish. Fresh bay leaves are a very elegant herb, with an attractive pine attitude, a hint of cooling camphor, and notes of green grass and citrus. If they're left whole and boiled for too long, all of this disappears, but if the leaves are chopped very finely, and cooked for just a few minutes or slightly longer, all those wonderful characteristics shine through (see tomato salad, p. 176). The same method can be used with other robust herbs, such as rosemary, sage, and thyme. In summary, if fresh herbs and flowers are cooked for a very short time, at a high temperature, the aromatic substances will be more lively and aesthetic. But once again, it all depends on the aroma profile you want a dish to have.

ACIDITY IN FOOD

I'm a great fan of acidity in food, whether it comes from fresh citrus, dried loomi, fresh pomegranates, sumac, vinegar, sour yogurt, hibiscus flowers, freshly squeezed fruit juice, or fruit juice that's cooked down to a thick syrup without any added sugar. They all give food an edge, and make it more interesting, because the acidity cleanses, and creates calm and order on your tongue. Acid can also be used to remedy a dish that's been over-seasoned.

SUMMER AND WINTER

Summer is the ideal time to fall head over heels in love with flowers and herbs. When they're in season and taste their best, I'm always happy to overdo both the amount and range of fresh flowers and herbs. I can't get enough. I pig out and don't think about what it costs, because I can just go out in the garden, and cut some more, or cut some other flower or herb. I also know it won't last. When dried, fresh herbs and flowers lose much of their aromas. Their water content can be as high as ninety percent, so no matter what you do, drying puts an end to some of the most interesting aromas. I rarely use dried herbs, though there are a few exceptions, such as cinnamon leaves. In winter, I use more spice, to compensate for the freshness that's no longer available. Spices are, and will always be, my favorite tools in the kitchen. They are my special effects and never disappoint. They also challenge and frustrate me, because they possess the largest and most unusual range of aromatic compounds that exists.

GREEN SPICES—EDGE AND ATTITUDE

If you've never tasted a fresh green seed of bronze fennel, coriander, or caraway, taken straight from the plant, you can look forward to experiencing an intense roller coaster ride into the wonderful world of aromatic substances. These unripe green seeds lend a thrilling, heavy, and exaggerated aroma to food. As long as you don't use too much, they'll provide an interesting energy to dishes that lack edge and attitude. Their aromatic compounds are like an unruly teenager, but as soon as the seeds are ripened by the sun and subsequently dried, they acquire a more balanced and mature character. The texture of unripe green spices is crisp and crunchy. They can be added, whole or coarsely chopped, to salads and fruit chutneys, as well as to egg, potato, rice, and pasta dishes. Or, brew a pot of tea with them, so you can get to know them first.

TIME HAS THE ABILITY TO MATURE THE EXPRESSION OF INGREDIENTS, AND CREATE PEACE, BALANCE AND HARMONY

USING CHILI

Invented by American chemist Wilbur Scoville in 1912, the international Scoville scale measures a chili's capsaicin content, which is the source of its strength. The Scoville scale goes from zero to sixteen million Scoville, with the number indicating how many times the capsaicin must be diluted with water to neutralize the chili. By using the Scoville scale—you can find it on the Internet—in combination with your own common sense and gut feeling, you can quickly get a clear grasp of and navigate smoothly between all sorts of fresh, dried, and smoked chilis. Up to eighty percent of a chili's strength can come from its seeds and membranes, so it's easy to make adjustments

by either keeping or removing these, and using only the flesh. But this advice should be tempered with caution, as there can be significant variations in both directions, depending entirely on the variety, temperature, climate, soil, cultivation method, and in particular, ripeness, all of which can affect the insistent strength of a chili. If you find it hard to get a handle on the jumble of fresh, dried, and smoked chili varieties, pickled or smoked chipotle chilis in adobo sauce, which are available in cans and jars, are a good place to start. You'll find them familiar, because when fresh jalapeño chilis are dried and smoked, they switch identities, and are called chipotle chilis. It was actually that taste that originally made me fall madly in love with chili.

MAKE YOUR OWN CHILI FLAKES

I use chili flakes instead of freshly ground black pepper in most of my recipes. They are used sparingly, as a 'spark,' and have a relatively neutral fragrance and taste compared to black peppercorns, but provide a warm, uplifting feeling to food. In fall and winter, I use mild or medium-hot smoked chilis that have deep and mature warm earthy notes, such as ancho, mulato, chipotle, and pasilla, because they go very well with root vegetables, cabbage, pumpkins, apples, and pears. In spring and summer, I mostly avoid the smoked varieties, and instead use mild or medium-hot chilis, such as serrano, jalapeño, Rocotillo, poblano, and Anaheim. They suit the seasons' tender, crunchy green leaves and vegetables. You can use all sorts of dried chilis to make flakes, but you will find the finest and most interesting kinds when traveling and visiting local food markets. What to do: Carefully twist off the stems of the dried chilis—wear gloves if you have sensitive skin—then roll the chilis between your fingers, so all the seeds fall out. Save the seeds for later and discard the membranes. If dirty, wipe the skin of the chilis with a damp cloth then break the chilis into several pieces. Heat a pan over high heat and gently dry-roast the chilis until they soften and start to smell lovely. This takes no more than thirty

ACIDITY GIVES FOOD AN EDGE AND MAKES IT MORE INTERESTING, BECAUSE IT CLEANSES, AND CREATES CALM AND ORDER ON YOUR TONGUE

to sixty seconds if the pan is hot, but be careful that the chilis don't burn or develop black spots. As soon as the chilis have cooled off, they'll turn crisp again, and can be roughly chopped on a cutting board. Put them, along with the reserved seeds, in a food processor, and blend until you have a coarse mixture in which both the seeds and the flesh are still visible. Or, use an electric coffee grinder to blend the mixture to a fine powder. The aromas that emanate can be quite fierce, so keep your distance, or you might have a violent coughing fit. Homemade chili flakes should be stored in a tightly sealed container, in a cool and dry spot, where they'll keep for months.

WINTER
ROOTS

CARROT

GLAZED CARROTS

800 g (1 ¾ lb) carrots without green tops

CHARACTER

An exotic and elegant blend; sharp, sour, bitter, and fresh.

VARIATIONS

The aromatic blend can also be used with other vegetables, seafood, or meat.

AROMATIC BLEND #9

1 (10 g) loomi (dried lime) (see p. 279)
100 g (3 ½ oz) drained yogurt (min. 10 % fat)
10 g (⅓ oz) fresh cilantro

Cold-pressed olive oil, for frying
Sea salt

New, whole carrots with a diameter of less than 2 cm (¾ in) need just 25 to 30 minutes in a hot frying pan. In winter, when carrots are obviously larger, they can be baked in a 230°C (450°F) oven for about 35 minutes, or cut into smaller pieces and fried. I feel there's something very special about pan-frying, especially when you put time and effort into making sure the vegetables get a smooth, golden, and caramelized surface. You can add a little honey for sweetness, and the cilantro can be replaced with mint, parsley, or dill.

AROMATIC BLEND

Crush the loomi with the lower part of your palm or something heavy. Put the crushed loomi in an electric coffee grinder and grind to a fine powder. Put the yogurt and cilantro in separate bowls, and set aside until needed. Durability: Use immediately. Makes 120 ml (½ cup).

CARROTS

Peel the carrots. Heat a large frying pan over high heat and add a little cold-pressed olive oil. Sauté the carrots, turning, for

15 minutes, or until they develop an even golden color. Add all but a pinch of the powdered loomi and season with sea salt. Continue cooking the carrots for 10 minutes, or until tender but still al dente. Top the carrots with the yogurt and cilantro, sprinkle with the reserved loomi powder, and serve immediately.

SEASON: All year round
Starter or side dish for 4

HORSERADISH / CASHEW / DILL / COCONUT FLOUR / CORIANDER SEED / LEMON JUICE / BROWN MUSTARD SEED / BUTTER / TURMERIC ROOT / CAYENNE / CREAM / FENUGREEK

CELERIAC

CELERIAC CURRY

1 celeriac without greens (1 kg / 2 ¼ lb)

CHARACTER

A fragrant, crunchy, pungent, and exotic blend with subtle nutty notes and a slight curry attitude.

VARIATIONS

The aromatic blend can also be used with potatoes, root vegetables, pasta dishes, poultry, fish, or shellfish, and as a topping for rice and grain dishes.

AROMATIC BLEND #10

60 g (3 tbsp) cashews or cashew nut butter
2 g (1 tsp) whole coriander seeds
1.3 g (½ tsp) whole fenugreek seeds
15 g (1 ½ tbsp) coconut flour
8 g (1 tbsp) finely grated fresh turmeric with peel
8 g (2 tsp) whole brown mustard seeds
0.3 g (⅛ tsp) ground cayenne pepper
40 g (1 ⅖ oz) unsalted butter
300 ml (1 ¼ cups) water or reserved celeriac water
120 ml (½ cup) heavy cream
30 ml (2 tbsp) freshly squeezed lemon juice
20 g (4 tbsp) finely grated fresh horseradish
Sea salt

30 g (2 tbsp) finely chopped fresh dill (topping)

This vegetable curry is mellow, gentle, highly fragrant, and ultra-creamy. It should be simmered only briefly to keep the aromas light and lively. Cut the celeriac into very large cubes, so its juiciness, texture, and unusual artichoke-like flavor can be fully experienced. For an even tastier dish, cook the celeriac first, and use the water from boiling it to make the aromatic blend. If you have some cooked chicken on hand, it can be folded in to turn this into a main dish.

AROMATIC BLEND

Put the cashews, coriander seeds, and fenugreek seeds in an electric coffee grinder or mortar and pestle and grind to a fine powder. Put the powder in a small bowl, add the coconut flour, turmeric, mustard seeds, and cayenne pepper and whisk to combine. In a medium saucepan over medium-high heat, melt the butter. Add the spice mixture and sauté for 2–3 minutes. Add the water (or the reserved celeriac water) and simmer, stirring, for 5 minutes, or until slightly thickened. Add the cream, lemon juice, and horseradish, season with sea salt, and bring to a boil. Reduce the heat and simmer for 2–3 minutes, or until creamy. Keep hot. Durability: Use the same day. Makes 475 ml (2 cups).

CELERIAC

Peel the celeriac (the cleaned weight should be approx. 800 g / 1 ¾ lb) and cut into 2 cm (¾ in) cubes. Put the celeriac in a large saucepan and add just enough boiling water to cover. Do not salt the water. Cover and bring to a boil. Continue boiling for 3–5 minutes, or until the celeriac is tender but still al dente. Pour the celeriac water off, reserving it for the aromatic blend, if desired. Fold the celeriac into the hot aromatic blend and boil for a few minutes then add the finely chopped dill and serve.

SEASON: September–March
Starter or side dish for 4

CREAM/MILK/BUTTER/ SAFFRON/BASIL/FENNEL SEED/PISTACHIOS

POTATO

SUMMER MASHED POTATOES

1 kg (2 ¼ lb) floury potatoes

CHARACTER

A warm, mild, creamy, and rich blend that's feminine and delicate with subtle notes of pistachio and anise.

VARIATIONS

The aromatic blend can also be used with root vegetables and pasta dishes, or as a creamy sauce over fish and seafood, poultry, meat, or vegetables.

AROMATIC BLEND #11

1.5 g (1½ tsp) whole fennel seeds
120 g (4 ¼ oz) unsalted butter
100 ml (7 tbsp) whole milk
80 ml (5 tbsp) heavy cream
A pinch of saffron threads
25 g (3 tbsp) finely chopped pistachios, plus more for topping
10 g (2 tbsp) finely chopped fresh basil, plus more for topping

25 g (5 tsp) coarse sea salt (for the potatoes)
2 (225 g / ½ lb) ripe peaches (topping)

I have an obsession with mashed potatoes, and therefore have no scruples in using new potatoes from the garden in August to make mash. In summer, peaches and apricots make interesting toppings. In winter, you can replace them with ripe apples and pears. You can also use parsley, sage, or lemon thyme instead of basil. The saffron can be replaced with freshly grated turmeric root, not because of its color, though it is delightful, but because the flavor suits the other ingredients extremely well. If you have any mashed potatoes left over, they can be baked as a gratin in a preheated 245°C (475°F) oven until the charming crust is crispy and golden brown. Or, make a fish pie by putting fish at the bottom and mash on top. If you serve the mashed potatoes as a side dish, you don't necessarily need the topping.

AROMATIC BLEND

Heat a small frying pan over high heat. Add the fennel seeds and dry-roast for 5–15 seconds, or until fragrant and beginning to take on color. Immediately put the fennel in an electric coffee grinder or mortar and pestle and grind to a fine powder. Put the powder in a small saucepan, along with the butter, milk, cream, and saffron. Warm over high heat until the butter melts then turn off the heat and add the pistachios (25 g / 3 tbsp) and basil (10 g / 2 tbsp). Keep hot. Durability: Use immediately, while still hot. Makes 300 ml (1 ¼ cups).

POTATOES

Peel the potatoes and put them in a large pot. Cover with cold water, add the coarse sea salt (25 g / 5 tsp), and bring to a boil. Reduce the heat to low and simmer, covered, for 15–25 minutes, or until a sharp knife can go all the way through the potatoes without any resistance. Do not overcook the potatoes. Drain the potatoes, return them to the pot, and place over high heat. Cook, shaking the pan and stirring, so the potatoes don't stick, for 1–2 minutes, or until the rest of the water steams off the potatoes. Run the potatoes through a food mill or potato ricer and put them in a medium bowl. Add all but 4–6 tbsp of the hot aromatic blend and gently stir until combined and creamy (there's no need to add extra sea salt). Serve the mashed potatoes, topped with peaches cut into chunks, pistachios, basil, and perhaps a little of the reserved hot aromatic blend.

A NOTE ON THE MASHED POTATOES

There are many methods for achieving that totally magical, airy, and creamy mashed potato consistency, but the secret is to work the mash as little as possible. The less stirring, the lighter the texture, as all that stirring affects the starch and makes the mash heavy and sometimes elastic. For the airiest mash, use a potato ricer or a food mill. Out come the loveliest spaghetti-shaped strands, and if you gently stir them together with the preheated mixture of butter, milk, and cream, you'll be closer than you realize to the dreamiest mashed potatoes. If you pour the milk mixture in cold, the temperature of the potatoes will be lowered, and they'll need more stirring.

I boil potatoes with plenty of coarse sea salt in the water and never need to add any additional salt later. The boiling gives the sea salt a mellower, rounder, and more natural taste, and also prevents the potatoes from falling apart because of too much water or overcooking. I keep my potatoes whole. If you cut them into small cubes they will naturally cook faster, but they will also absorb too much water, because there are more open surfaces.

SEASON: All year round
Starter or side dish for 4

HAZELNUT/ALLSPICE/
SEA SALT FLAKES/CEYLON
CINNAMON/MAPLE SYRUP/
OLIVE OIL/MACE/LEMON
JUICE/SMOKED PAPRIKA

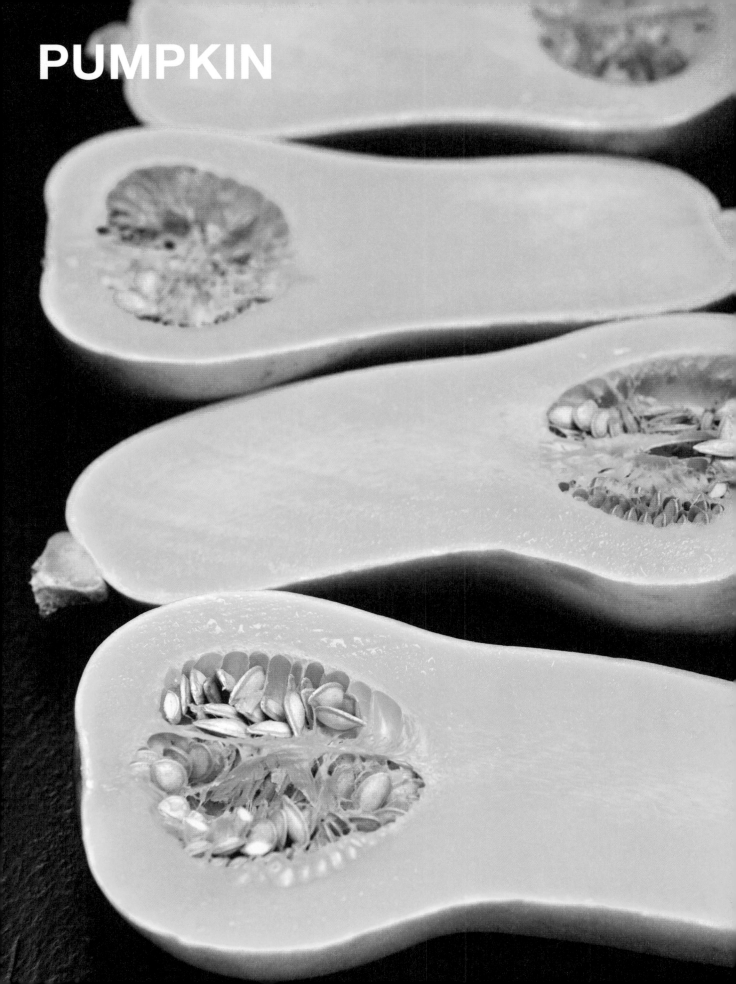

PUMPKIN

SMOKY CARAMELIZED PUMPKIN

1 kg (2 ¼ lb) pumpkin (butternut squash)

CHARACTER

An addictive, warm, fresh, sweet, and sour blend, with subtle yet rich smoky notes.

VARIATIONS

The aromatic blend can also be used to glaze fried or roasted meat, poultry, fish, or shellfish, as well as with all kinds of vegetables, or as a salad dressing.

AROMATIC BLEND #12

1.25 cm (½ in) (1 g) Ceylon cinnamon stick
4 (0.8 g) whole allspice berries
0.8 g (½ tsp) whole mace or nutmeg
40 g (1 ⅖ oz) hazelnuts
1 g (½ tsp) sweet smoked paprika, plus more for topping
45 ml (3 tbsp) freshly squeezed lemon juice
45 ml (3 tbsp) maple syrup
30 ml (2 tbsp) cold-pressed olive oil
Sea salt flakes

Pumpkin shows its full potential when peeled and roasted at a high temperature. You'll be rewarded with a dish that's generously caramelized, has a fantastically creamy texture—it's almost like candy— and tastes rich and smoky.

AROMATIC BLEND

Put the cinnamon, allspice berries, and mace in a mortar and pestle and grind to a fine powder. Add the hazelnuts and grind them finely. Put the mixture in a small bowl, add the smoked paprika, lemon juice, maple syrup, and cold-pressed olive oil and stir until well combined. Durability: Use the same day. Makes 150 ml (10 tbsp).

PUMPKIN

Peel the squash with a broad potato peeler then cut in half lengthwise and scrape out the seeds and stringy flesh with a spoon. Cut the squash flesh crosswise into uniform slices, 4 cm (1½ in) thick. Put the squash slices in a parchment paper–lined roasting pan that fits them snugly in a single layer and roast in a preheated 220°C (420°F) oven for 30 minutes. Pour the aromatic blend evenly over the squash, making sure it stays on top and doesn't just drip down to the bottom of the pan; otherwise, it will burn off. Roast, without flipping, for 20–30 minutes, or until the squash is golden and lightly caramelized on the surface. Sprinkle with the sea salt flakes and possibly some smoked paprika.

SEASON: September–December
Starter or side dish for 4–6

LEMON JUICE/TAHINI/RED ONION/WATER/OLIVE OIL/ SEA SALT/BLACK PEPPER/ CUMIN/CHILI/SPEARMINT

SALSIFY

PAN-FRIED SALSIFY

1 kg (2 ¼ lb) salsify

CHARACTER
A fresh, creamy, and quite tart blend that's full of contrast, and has deep, warm, sweet, and nutty notes.

VARIATIONS
The aromatic blend can also be used as a dip with raw vegetables or French fries, as a salad dressing (if diluted), or as a spread on flatbread and in sandwiches. It can also be poured over fatty fish and baked in the oven.

AROMATIC BLEND #13
4.5 g (1½ tsp) whole cumin seeds
Cold-pressed olive oil, for frying
130 g (4 ½ oz) finely chopped red onion
A pinch of chili flakes
75 g (5 tbsp) unsalted tahini (sesame paste)
100 ml (7 tbsp) boiling water
45 ml (3 tbsp) freshly squeezed lemon juice
10 g (2 tbsp) finely chopped fresh spearmint, plus more for topping
Sea salt
Freshly ground black pepper

Seeds from 1 large pomegranate (topping)

This dish has a lot of dominant sharpness, so it's important that the red onions and the salsify be cooked until golden brown, crispy, and caramelized. Then you will experience plenty of sweetness and a nutty aroma that complements the many tangy notes already present in the dish.

AROMATIC BLEND
Put the cumin seeds in an electric coffee grinder or mortar and pestle and grind to a fine powder. Heat a medium frying pan over medium heat and add a little cold-pressed olive oil. Add the cumin powder, along with the red onion and chili flakes, and sauté for 6–10 minutes, or until the red onions are golden brown, crispy, and caramelized. Remove from the heat. In a medium bowl, stir together the tahini and boiling water then add the hot onion mixture, along with the lemon juice and spearmint. Season with sea salt and freshly ground black pepper. The aromatic blend can easily be made a few hours ahead, and kept at room temperature. Durability: 6 days refrigerated. Makes 240 ml (1 cup).

SALSIFY
Peel the salsify and remove and discard the tops. Cut the salsify into uniform 1 cm (⅜ in) slices. Salsify quickly changes color to red-brown when exposed to oxygen, so it can make quite a mess. This has no effect on the appearance or taste—the salsify will change color again when cooked—so don't bother soaking it in lemon water.

Heat a large frying pan over medium heat and add a little cold-pressed olive oil. Sauté

the salsify, stirring frequently to ensure even browning, for 15 minutes, or until golden and crisp. Serve the salsify topped with the aromatic blend, fresh pomegranate seeds (approx. 175 g / ¾ cup), and spearmint.

A NOTE ON POMEGRANATES
Inside these grenade-like fruits are hundreds of small, attractive seeds that are bursting with sharp, juicy sweetness To get access to this ruby-red aromatic experience, place the pomegranate on a cutting board and cut a square on the top, around the stem and just penetrating the leathery rind. Next, make 4 cuts gently down the sides, from the top to the bottom of the fruit. Open up the fruit and take out the seeds. This method is easy and efficient, as it does not destroy the seeds and avoids getting splashes of red juice everywhere. Plus, you get only a few of the troublesome yellow membranes. The unique thing about pomegranate seeds is that eating them feels like a small explosion in your mouth—an effect that can be used to great effect in dishes that need a hint of sweet and fruity sharpness.

SEASON: October–March
Starter or side dish for 4

CAUGHT FROM THE SEA

LEMON GRASS / CUMIN / CILANTRO / CANE SUGAR / GARLIC / CHILI / FENNEL SEED / PEANUTS / SEA SALT / TOMATO / OLIVE OIL

MACKEREL

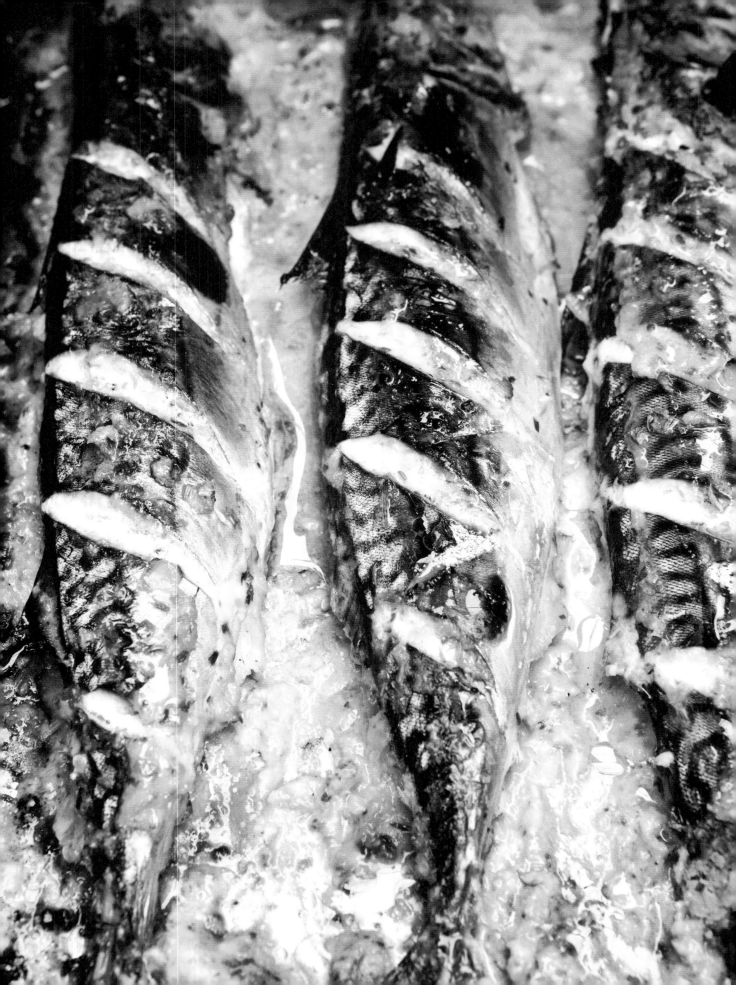

WHOLE ROASTED MACKEREL

4 whole cleaned mackerel (1 kg / 2 ¼ lb)

CHARACTER

A warm and refined Asian-inspired blend that's creamy and tart with nutty notes.

VARIATIONS

The aromatic blend can also be used when roasting or pan frying other fish, as well as seafood, lamb, and poultry (whole or fillet).

AROMATIC BLEND #14

2.8 g (1 tsp) whole cumin seeds
1.8 g (1 tsp) whole fennel seeds
1 (20 g) stalk lemon grass
200 g (7 oz) ripe yellow tomatoes
30 g (2½ tbsp) blanched, roasted, unsalted peanuts
5 (25 g) cloves garlic, peeled
1 (10 g) fresh yellow or red chili with seeds
10 g (⅓ oz) fresh cilantro or parsley
5 g (1 tsp) light cane sugar
15 ml (1 tbsp) cold-pressed olive oil
Sea salt

This is an aromatic, addictive, and really easy dish to make. Mackerel's dark, fatty meat is exceptionally tasty, but if it's not freshly caught, it will smell rancid and isn't worth wasting time on, so only make this dish when you can get hold of the freshest fish. To maximize the roasting juices, use a roasting pan that fits the mackerel snugly—if there is too much space around the fish, the aromatic blend may evaporate too quickly or even burn in the hot oven and then you won't have any sauce for serving.

AROMATIC BLEND

Heat a small frying pan over high heat. Add the cumin and fennel seeds and dry-roast for 5–15 seconds, or until fragrant and beginning to take on color. Immediately put the cumin and fennel seeds in an electric coffee grinder or mortar and pestle and grind to a fine powder.

Meanwhile, remove the dry, outermost leaves from the lemon grass. Trim the root, leaving it intact as much as possible, then use only 5 cm (2 in) of the lower, white part, and discard or reserve the dry top. Use a pestle to crush the lower, white part then finely chop it. Put the lemon grass in the mortar, add the ground spices, and grind until the mixture has a fine, even texture. Put this in a food processor or blender, along with the tomatoes, peanuts, garlic, chili, cilantro, light cane sugar, and cold-pressed olive oil. Season with sea salt and blend until smooth and glossy. Durability: 3 days refrigerated. Makes 300 ml (1 ¼ cups).

MACKEREL

Rinse the mackerel under cold running water and dry completely. Cut 3–4 deep incisions on both sides of each mackerel then arrange snugly in a roasting pan. Add the aromatic blend and rub it into the mackerel. Roast in a preheated 230°C (450°F) oven for 10–20 minutes, or until juicy, golden, and caramelized. Be careful not to overcook the mackerel or they will be too dry. If the fish needs more color on top, put it under the broiler for a few minutes. Add a little boiling water to the roasting pan, and scrape the bottom of the pan with a wooden spoon to release any stuck bits. Pour the juices over the mackerel when serving.

SEASON: May–September
Main dish for 4

POTATO/CAULIFLOWER/ HORSERADISH/SAFFRON/ OLIVE OIL/TARRAGON/ CREAM

MUSSEL

CREAMY MUSSEL SOUP

1 kg (2 ¼ lb) cleaned mussels

CHARACTER

A sweet, creamy, and mild herbal blend, with a refined almond aroma and elegant anise notes.

VARIATIONS

The aromatic blend can also be used with other shellfish, such as clams, as well as fish, poultry, or vegetables.

AROMATIC BLEND #15

200 g (7 oz) finely chopped cauliflower
200 g (7 oz) boiled, peeled potatoes, cut into thin (½ cm / ⅛ in) slices
10 g (2 tbsp) finely chopped fresh tarragon
10 g (2 tbsp) finely grated fresh horseradish
100 ml (7 tbsp) heavy cream
30 ml (2 tbsp) cold-pressed olive oil
A pinch of saffron threads

240 ml (1 cup) unfiltered apple juice, for steaming
Sea salt

The trick to this dish is to add the mussels, in a single layer, to a very hot, dry skillet. As soon as they start shaking vigorously, which should take less than a minute, you add unfiltered apple juice. This shocks the shellfish and they open within a few minutes. The result is mussels with the perfect texture. Another advantage of this cooking technique is that the mussels can be stored in the liquid overnight, and reheated without affecting their texture. The aromatic blend calls forth almond notes that taste fantastically good when combined with the mussel juices.

AROMATIC BLEND

Put the cauliflower, potatoes, tarragon, horseradish, cream, cold-pressed olive oil, and saffron in a medium bowl and toss to combine. Durability: Use the same day. Makes 720 ml (3 cups).

MUSSELS

Heat a large skillet until very hot then add the mussels in 1 even layer. As soon as the mussels start to shake vigorously—this takes less than 1 minute—add the apple juice—it will splash and spit violently—and cover the skillet. Cook the mussels for 3–5 minutes, or until they open. Discard any mussels that don't open. Remove the mussels from their shells. Set the mussels aside and discard the shells. Pour about 240 ml (1 cup) of the mussel cooking liquid through a paper coffee filter or fine-mesh sieve into a saucepan. Add the aromatic blend, season with sea salt, and bring to a boil. Add the steamed mussels, boil for 5 minutes, and serve.

SEASON: October–March
Starter for 4-6

ANISE SEED / LEMON ZEST / WHITE SUGAR / TARRAGON / SEA SALT / FENNEL SEED

SALMON

GRAVLAX

1 fillet salmon with skin (1.4 kg / 3 lb)

CHARACTER
This blend is classic, simple, feminine, warm, and pure; it's layered with licorice-anise notes.

VARIATIONS
The aromatic blend can also be used for curing other fish, as well as marinating poultry or meat

AROMATIC BLEND #16
2 g (1 tsp) whole fennel seeds
1.3 g (½ tsp) whole anise seeds
200 g (7 oz) white sugar
200 g (7 oz) fine sea salt
20 g (3½ tbsp) finely grated lemon zest
10 g (2 tbsp) finely chopped fresh tarragon

Curing brings out the best in fatty fish like salmon. The texture becomes amazingly velvety and the taste deep and elegant. Every two weeks, I cure my own salmon fillets. It's easy and inexpensive, and the results are sophisticated and exceptionally tasty—far better than anything you can buy in the stores. Remember that the salmon must be absolutely fresh, and the sea salt fine (not coarse), of a very good quality, and preferably unrefined. A tasty option is to pan-fry or oven-bake thick slices of gravlax.

AROMATIC BLEND
Put the fennel and anise seeds in an electric coffee grinder or mortar and pestle and grind to a medium-fine powder. Put the powder in a large bowl, add the white sugar, sea salt, lemon zest, and tarragon and toss to combine. Durability: 5–7 days at room temperature. Makes 430 g (15 oz).

SALMON
DAY 1: Remove any bones from the salmon, pat it dry, and arrange, skin side down, in a stainless steel or glass roasting pan that fits it snugly. Sprinkle the aromatic blend over the salmon, cover with a piece of parchment paper or a lid, and refrigerate for 24 hours. As it slowly dissolves, some of the aromatic blend will slide off the salmon onto the bottom of the pan. Every 12 hours, flip the salmon and spoon the aromatic blend over the fillet again. Con-

tinue to cure for another 2 days, or until the salmon acquires a velvety texture.

If you're in doubt about whether the salmon is ready, scrape some of the aromatic blend off, cut a few thin slices, and taste the fish. Don't judge by the first outer slices, as these will have a more intense taste. As a rule of thumb, 2–3 days is a suitable length of time for small and medium sides of salmon.

DAY 2–3: After 48–72 hours, take the salmon out of the refrigerator. Use a knife to scrape off the aromatic blend and discard. The finished gravlax will keep for 4–5 days in a tightly sealed container in the refrigerator. To serve, cut into thin slices.

SEASON: All year round
Starter for 4–8

APPLE CIDER VINEGAR / SEA SALT / TURMERIC ROOT / HIBISCUS FLOWERS / CHILI / LEMON GRASS / GARLIC

SHRIMP

PAN-FRIED
SHRIMP SALAD

400 g (14 oz) whole raw shrimp with shells

CHARACTER

A fresh, spicy yet sweet blend with subtle, warm citrus notes and an Asian attitude.

VARIATIONS

The aromatic blend can also be used with other fish and shellfish, such as mackerel, salmon, squid, cod, and mussels, as well as salads and dishes made with vegetables, meat, pulses, and grains.

AROMATIC BLEND #17

1 (20 g) stalk lemon grass
2 (10 g) cloves garlic
8 g (1 tbsp) finely grated fresh turmeric with peel
½ (8 g) fresh yellow or red chili, with seeds, coarsely chopped
2 (6.5 g) whole hibiscus flowers (see p. 223)
30 ml (2 tbsp) unfiltered apple cider vinegar
2 g (½ tsp) sea salt

Cold-pressed peanut oil, for frying
400 g (14 oz) coarsely chopped romaine lettuce (topping)
150 ml (10 tbsp) water (topping)

This is an easy-to-make salad that's fresh, filling, and elegant. Choose lettuce that's sweet and juicy, with a crunchy texture that won't soften too much when sautéed. Because the dish is only in the pan for a few minutes, the aromatic blend must be chopped and ground very finely, using a mortar and pestle—a blender won't do—so the lemon grass doesn't dominate. For this same reason, use only the lower white part of the lemon grass, which is where most of the flavor is anyway. You can save the green top and add it to herbal teas or slow-cooked soups and stews. If you like coconut, try adding a little creamy coconut milk (approx. 60 ml / 4 tbsp), at the very end, when adding the lettuce.

AROMATIC BLEND

Remove the dry, outermost leaves from the lemon grass. Trim the root, leaving it intact as much as possible, then use only 5 cm (2 in) of the lower, white part, and discard or reserve the dry green top. Use a pestle to crush the lower, white part then finely chop it. Put the lemon grass in the mortar, add the garlic, turmeric, chili, and hibiscus flowers and grind until the mixture has a fine, even texture. Add the apple cider vinegar and sea salt. If possible, let stand 1–2 days before using. The aromatic blend will develop more flavor over time. Durability: 5 days refrigerated. Makes 75 ml (⅓ cup).

SHRIMP

Peel the shrimp then discard and remove the intestine with a sharp knife (the cleaned weight should be approx. 250 g / 8¾ oz). In a medium bowl, toss the shrimp with the aromatic blend and marinate at room temperature for 1–2 hours. Heat a very large frying pan over high heat and add a little cold-pressed peanut oil. Sauté the shrimp and the aromatic blend for less than 1 minute, or until the shrimp turn a dark golden caramel color. Immediately transfer to a plate. Put the frying pan back over high heat, add the romaine lettuce and water, and sauté for 10–15 seconds, or until the lettuce collapses but is still crunchy. Turn off the heat, add the shrimp, toss to combine, and serve immediately.

SEASON: All year round
Large starter for 4-6

ANCHO CHILI / OREGANO / CEYLON CINNAMON / BLACK PEPPERCORN / APPLE JUICE / CUMIN / COCONUT SUGAR / GARLIC

SQUID

GRILLED SQUID SALAD

800 g (1¾ lb) small squid

CHARACTER

A warm, deep, and aromatic blend with sweet, caramelized notes that call forth memories of smoking BBQs.

VARIATIONS

The aromatic blend can also be used with octopus and other seafood, as well as meat, poultry, and vegetables.

AROMATIC BLEND #18

1 (20 g) dried ancho chili
2.5 cm (1 in) (2 g) Ceylon cinnamon stick
20 (1.5 g) whole black peppercorns
1.5 g (½ tsp) whole cumin seeds
3 (15 g) cloves garlic
6 g (1½ tsp) coconut sugar
2.5 g (1 tbsp) fresh oregano
200 ml (13 tbsp) unfiltered apple juice

500 g (18 oz) cucumber, cut into thick wedges (topping)
A handful of fresh cilantro (topping)
Sea salt

This warm salad has a nice balance of sweetness, acidity, and smoke, getting its smokiness from both the aromatic blend and the use of the grill. The sauce is very aromatic but not gaspingly hot. If you cannot find ancho chili, replace it with 7 g (1 tsp) finely chopped chipotle chili in adobo sauce. Try to get hold of small squid, which tend to have better flavor and a more delicate texture than larger squid. Additional ingredients, such as potatoes, beans, tomatoes, and root vegetables, can be added to turn this into a more substantial dish.

AROMATIC BLEND

Carefully twist the stem off the dried ancho chili. Roll the chili between your fingers, so that all the seeds fall out. Discard the seeds and membranes and break the chili into a couple of pieces (there should be approx. 15 g / ½ oz cleaned chili). Heat a small frying pan over high heat. Add the chili pieces and dry-roast for less than 30 seconds, or until fragrant and soft; be careful not to burn the chili. Put the chili in a bowl, add just enough boiling water to cover, and let stand for 20–30 minutes, or until completely soft. Strain the chili, reserving the water for later use.

Put the pan back over high heat. Add the cinnamon, black peppercorns, and cumin seeds and dry-roast for 5–15 seconds, or until fragrant and beginning to take on color. Immediately put the spices in an electric coffee grinder or a mortar and pestle and grind to a fine powder. Put the powder, along with the soaked chili, garlic, coconut sugar, and oregano in a food processor and blend until the mixture has a smooth, fine texture. Add the apple juice and blend until smooth. If the aromatic blend is too thick, gradually add a little of the reserved chili water.

Put the aromatic blend in a small saucepan and bring to a boil. Reduce the heat and simmer for 4–5 minutes. The aromatic blend may be very strongly flavored, but keep in mind that it will mellow once it's cooked with the squid. Pour the sauce into a clean preserves jar. Durability: 7 days refrigerated. Makes 240 ml (1 cup).

SQUID

Clean the squid by gently pulling off the heads, so that the innards follow. Be careful not to puncture the ink sac! Cut the tentacles as close as possible to the eyes; discard the eyes and innards. Check that the small hard beak does not remain on the tentacles. Inside the body is a transparent skeleton, which is easily removed by grasping the pointed edge of the body and pulling it out. Remove the two fins and cut the body so that it can be opened into 1 large piece (if the squid are small, keep them whole). There should be approx. 600 g (21 oz) cleaned bodies and tentacles. Rinse both the bodies and the tentacles in water and dry them thoroughly. Cut the bodies in a crisscross fashion with a sharp knife (this is not necessary if they are small), then toss with 180–240 ml (¾–1 cup) of the aromatic blend and marinate at room temperature for at least 30 minutes and up to 2 hours; reserve the remaining aromatic blend for later use.

Preheat a grill to hot. Grill the squid, without adding fat and flipping once, for 2–4 minutes, or until the squid turns from translucent to white, which means it's tender. Be careful not to overcook the squid, which can quickly turn dry and rubbery. Put the squid in a large bowl, add the cucumber, cilantro, and possibly a little of the reserved aromatic blend. Toss to combine, season with sea salt, and serve immediately.

SEASON: April–June
Starter or side dish for 4

A DAY IN PARIS.
TALKING TO
DENNIS PAPHITIS

Dennis Paphitis is an Australian-born, Greek Cypriot. He is best known as the founder of Aesop, a highly respected botanical skincare company with more than 200 signature stores worldwide. When I first met Dennis in New York, I had just launched Taste of a Scent, my line of botanical extracts for spring water. I saw Dennis as a pioneering explorer of a road I had yet to take and I wanted his advice and guidance. I also recognized that we share a similar approach to botanical perception, while each having our own distinct aesthetic signature.

During our talk, I thought to myself, that with Dennis' striking story and background, it would be intriguing for my readers— not to mention me—if he were to interview me for this book.

SPICES ACT LIKE BRIDGES, MAKING IT POSSIBLE TO ACCESS THE OTHER INGREDIENTS

Dennis suggested we catch up in Paris, so I packed my suitcase with aromatic blends to make our supper, plus one of my fruit salamis as a present. When I arrived, Dennis was energetic, efficient, and still wearing shorts in December! He showed me his favorite Parisian street for food shopping, where I picked up the key ingredients for our small feast. In return for his generosity and kindness, I cooked recipes from this book, while Dennis brought these questions to the table.

YOUR APPROACH TO COOKING SEEMS MORE LIKE PAINTING A PICTURE, IN WHICH A CANVAS IS FIRST PREPARED AND THEN BUILT UPON. IS THAT THE CASE?
That's correct. I don't think about cooking or ingredients—I think about spices! For me, fruits and vegetables are like spices. That is, they are tools with their own colors—and without identity, origin, or history—that can be mixed together to create unique nuances. And cooking with this mindset leads to completely new and different combination possibilities.

WAS THERE A MOMENT WHEN AN INGREDIENT SANG OUT TO YOU AND IGNITED THIS PROCESS OF EXPLORATION?
When I fall head over heels in love with a spice, my mind goes on standby. I can't remember exactly when this first happened, because I more or less feel that way about everything—not just food. Of course, I've had special experiences associated with particular spices. It must be more than twenty years since I first tasted Ceylon cinnamon in a Moroccan lamb tagine. It was liberating to discover that sweet spices like cinnamon—and, for that matter, other sweet spices—are such an elegant accompaniment to meat. Today, I know that Ceylon cinnamon and cassia cinnamon are like night and day, but there was a time when I thought that cinnamon tastes like cinnamon, ginger tastes like ginger, mint tastes like mint, etc. There are many varieties of spices and herbs that share the same name, but the majority are mediocre in terms of their aromatic potential. And very few are phenomenal. It requires detective work, in which you can never be absolutely certain. You have to be very observant and use your instincts, time after time.

TO WHAT DEGREE DO YOU BELIEVE THAT GREAT FOOD CAN HEAL BROKEN SPIRITS?
We know that taste and scent experiences are specifically associated with our behaviors, moods, and emotions. If, for example, I haven't had spices or herbs for a few days, or haven't experienced something that tastes good, I become

discouraged, restless, dissatisfied, irritated, and very difficult to be around. So, the answer is yes, but if food is going to heal our souls, the combination and quality of the ingredients is crucial. I am convinced that the body can detect and register quality and that it becomes confused and stressed when exposed to the opposite. The use of spices in food is absolutely essential. They evoke vitality in the form of chemical reactions that occur when those spices are mixed with other ingredients. Spices act like bridges, making it possible to access the other ingredients, so you can experience a greater aroma and flavor potential. This vitality is of exceptionally high sensory quality, and can embrace the soul and help it to heal. There's no doubt about it. But, as I said, it's the combination and quality that make all the difference.

SOME AROMA AND FLAVOR COMBINATIONS, SUCH AS TURMERIC, CUMIN, AND GINGER, GO NATURALLY WELL TOGETHER YET DON'T SEEM TO BE COMMONLY USED. WHY DO YOU THINK THIS IS THE CASE?

It's a complicated business to compose something that both feels and tastes natural. It's not something you experience every day. And perhaps that is also for the best. Chance may, in fact, be the best way. It's obvious that when ingredients go naturally well together, they make a greater impression on you. Different botanical forces come into play, allowing certain ingredients to step into character. This kind of nourishment for body and soul has a different quality, and is on another level, so it has a unique effect. Food that is merely tasty and filling doesn't stimulate nearly as much, or strike the nerves in quite the same way. A good meal, in my view, should always contain a dimension—a fleeting irritation—that the tongue and the nose have a hard time accepting. The example you mention may be because turmeric and ginger belong to the same botanical family, and thus often create peace and harmony when combined in a dish. Cumin is also one of the easiest spices to work with in the kitchen. If you dry-roast the seeds and add them in relatively small amounts, they can improve almost any dish.

WHAT DOES 'WORK ENERGY' MEAN TO YOU?

Work energy is my most precious possession and greatest love. I would sacrifice everything I have for it. It's also the only time when I feel there's meaning in what I do. When I work with spices, it's like playing chess. Every time I make a move, it changes the rules, and produces endless potential combinations. The challenges I face just bowl me over. I find myself in deep water and maximally stimulated, because the work requires such extreme focus, discipline, and imagination. Right there, an indescribable energy arises that I don't experience from anything else.

HOW DO YOU BEGIN WORKING WITH AN UNKNOWN SPICE?

I try to ignore everything that's previously been written about the spice, no matter how relevant or useful it may be. For me, one of the greatest joys is not knowing precisely what I'm getting into—it's the joy of anticipation. It's like riding a bike for the first time. You have no idea whether you are going to stay up or fall down. The first thing I do, whether I am working with herbs, roots, bark, flowers, or seeds, is pour boiling water over them. Then, for the next week, I observe how the smell and taste develop. Is it best immediately, on the day itself, or does it improve and develop by being allowed to stand a little longer? Then I start cooking, using the spice sparingly and generously, in sweet and savory dishes. And then I start doing research. Sooner or later, after a few months, I will have found a place for it, though that doesn't mean it will always be in that place. If the spice is suddenly affected by something else and something new arises that I didn't register the first time, then I start all over again.

WHEN I WORK WITH SPICES, IT'S LIKE PLAYING CHESS

SINCE YOU INTRODUCED ME TO LOOMI, I'VE BECOME A CONVERT. HOW DO I FIND THE BEST QUALITY, AND HOW SHOULD I STORE IT?

Loomi is a citrus fruit in a class of its own. Everyone really ought to have loomi standing beside the salt and pepper, because it is just so useful. You can buy loomi in Middle Eastern markets, where it's cheap, or it's available online.

Loomi has a very stable aromatic intensity, so it's relatively easy to find good quality. It can be shrunken or spherical, but the shape has no impact on the quality, as long as the fruit is hard and intact, without cracks or holes. Loomi varies in color from brown to black and the darker it is, the more intense the fermented citrus flavor will be. The completely dark ones have a thinner shell, which makes them extra fragile. If you keep loomi in a cool, dry place, in a tightly sealed container, it can be enjoyed for years (p. 279).

WHAT IS YOUR PROCESS FOR CREATING EDIBLE AROMAS?

It's mostly spontaneous. Over the years, I've created a system that helps me reach my goals, but that's not what I begin with—it's more of an emergency solution. If I create an aromatic blend intuitively and it succeeds the first time, or if I discover something I haven't experienced before and which I can work on, then I know that the sensory quality will be more unique. It's not something I can explain; I just feel it. Still, I can describe the elements an aromatic blend must contain to make it interesting for me. First is tempo, or how quickly or slowly you experience the fragrance and flavor. Next, is dynamics, the number of ingredients—sometimes three is enough, other times eight might do it. Then there is rhythm, the combination of everything you experience on your tongue and in your nose. The rhythm should not be stable, but should swing, include breaks, and do something unexpected. It's a bit like music. And if the blend is not convincing enough, I think of Yin and Yang, opposites in harmony. It doesn't always work, but it's good to think about when you're mixing ingredients together. A blend also needs a hint of sweetness, acidity, something strong or stinging, and a little bitterness. But, as I said, I'd rather not think about all this when I'm just starting out the process.

TO WHAT DEGREE IS YOUR COOKING NORDIC-INSPIRED, AND HOW DID MIDDLE EASTERN FLAVORS COME TO FEATURE SO HEAVILY IN YOUR WORK?

I've never felt particularly Danish or Nordic, although I was born and raised in Denmark. I come from an unconventional home. My mother is a painter and ceramist, and traditional cuisine and food traditions—or, for that matter, even something as normal as lemons—were not part of my childhood. On the other hand, we ate according to the seasons. Everything was fresh and often seasoned with thyme and sage. My apprenticeship as a cook was in Danish/French nouvelle cuisine, so mustard, pepper, horseradish, dill, parsley, onion, vinegar, wine, lemon, vanilla, cream, and butter dominated the seasoning. But when I left London, in the mid-90s, after working as a chef for a couple of years, everything I learned was turned upside down thanks to Antony Worrall Thompson. Antony was officially my boss, but he also had the greatest influence on where I am today. When I was just twenty, he gave me the most important advice: "You won't find the answers you seek in other people. You have to find them and teach them to yourself." Antony introduced me to Moroccan lamb tagine with marinated lemons, saffron, cinnamon, and coriander and it was an experience that left a strong impression on me in more ways than one. So, no one taught me how to cook with spices, and I don't think of spices as Indian, Chinese, Moroccan, or Mexican. For me, they are timeless tools that I use to achieve my goals.

WHEN WE WENT TO THE MARKETS HERE IN PARIS, YOU SPENT 80 EUROS ON EXOTIC CITRUS. WHAT WAS THAT ABOUT? WHAT WILL YOU DO WITH ALL THAT FRUIT?

Citrus fruits are an iconic kind of seasoning. They contain large or small concentrations of mellow, floral sweetness in their flowers and leaves, cooling vital acidity in their juice, and deep, warming bitterness in their zest and white flesh. Over the past decade, I've used citrus fruits to create aroma extracts for Taste of a Scent. I've tried to capture their most interesting aspects, and unite that diversity in a simple aroma extract. So, when I see fresh yuzu, green bergamot, Buddha's hand, cédrat, Seville orange, and citrus varieties I'm not familiar with, I pounce, just as I did today. Winter is also peak season for citrus, so I always substitute lemon and orange zest with bergamot and Seville orange, because they contain more interesting aromatic compounds than the usual citrus varieties.

WHERE DID THE IDEA OF WARM SALAD DRESSING COME FROM? SPECIFICALLY, I'M CURIOUS ABOUT THE ONE YOU MADE FOR ME, WITH DATES, APPLE, SAFFRON, ENDIVE, AND HORSERADISH?

Pure chance. The weather was cold and rainy, so I chose a warm dressing. Also, I know that when you toss cool, crunchy lettuce leaves that are slightly thick with a warm salad dressing, it creates refinement. In the same week, a friend returning from Iran, brought me saffron that I used, along with orange flower water and other ingredients, to make an aromatic blend for perfumed peach sorbet. So, in my mind, I was already in the Middle East, in terms of scent and flavor. One thing led to another, and as chance would have it, when I needed some sweetness, I choose fresh dates instead of cane sugar. I mixed it all together, tasted it, and felt the dish lacked edge, that fleeting sense of irritation. So, I opened the fridge and there lay horseradish, which I quickly grated over the still-warm salad. Bingo! (p. 40)

IS APPLE CIDER VINEGAR AN IMPORTANT TOOL FOR YOU?

Yes, it has cult status in my kitchen. The taste of apple is, in general, fabulous when used as a spice and not as an ingredient. Unfiltered apple cider vinegar is fermented apple juice that's been turned into vinegar. It's an elegant blend of fruity sweetness, acidity, and light fermentation that is neither obvious nor dull. This makes it exceptionally useful in cooking. Plus, it works well in spicy dishes, where ordinary wine vinegar often seems rough and out of place. The taste of apple cider vinegar varies tremendously, especially due to the choice of apple varieties, so it requires a little detective work to find the good ones. If you like a little more sweetness in your apple cider vinegar, you can always reduce 200 ml (13 tbsp.) of freshly squeezed, unfiltered apple juice in a small saucepan until there is only 30 ml (2 tbsp.) left and the consistency looks syrupy. Pour the syrup into your bottle of apple cider vinegar and shake vigorously. Or, buy the slightly more expensive balsamic apple vinegar, which has more sweetness and less acidity.

THE GREAT FRUIT SALAMI—COULD YOU MAKE IT WITH PEAT WHISKEY?

Yes, whiskey would be a perfect choice. The smoky notes would certainly suit the fruit salami. Whiskey is quite nostalgic, and fills the scene with dominant notes like malt, caramel, leather, wood, peat, earth, cigar, and, in particular, a feeling of security. It goes very well with dried fruits, nuts, dark chocolate, Ceylon cinnamon, cloves, and allspice, which are all used in the salami. Unfortunately, it also means we must say goodbye to the light, green, botanical plant notes of aquavit and vodka, which have been added precisely to give the overall taste sensation some edge (p. 206).

WHY? WHAT MAKES YOU DO ALL THIS? WHEN DO YOU KNOW YOU'RE 'THERE'?

The feeling of freedom, a fast tempo, the perfect aroma moment, and the ultimate satisfaction. I'm fascinated by these perfect moments, because they contain authenticity, intensity, and quality nourishment for the body and soul. I'm attracted by a fast tempo in everything I spend my time doing. I've been like that since childhood. It's like a sport. When you're moving at high speed and doing your best work, there's no room for

AND ONCE IN A WHILE, THESE PERFECT AROMA MOMENTS ARISE, WHEN TIME STANDS STILL AND EVERYTHING MAKES SENSE

triviality and security, so you go through life feeling less worried and more focused. And once in a while, these perfect aroma moments arise, when time stands still and everything makes sense. I know exactly when it hits me—I feel joy and get goose bumps. When I get up in the morning, I expect to have the chance to experience a scent and a flavor, a moment that turns everything upside down.

MEAT
FROM
THE
COUNTRY

HONEY/LOOMI/BUTTER/ CHIPOTLE CHILI/CEYLON CINNAMON/LIME JUICE/ SEA SALT

CHICKEN

BAKED FLATTENED CHICKEN

1 whole chicken (1.5 kg / 3 ⅓ lb)

CHARACTER
A lightly smoky blend that's caramelized and full of sweetness, with unmistakable warmth and deep citrus notes.

VARIATIONS
The aromatic blend can also be used with pork, lamb, beef, seafood, and vegetables.

AROMATIC BLEND # 19
2 (20 g) loomi (dried lime) (see p. 279)
5 cm (2 in) (4 g) Ceylon cinnamon stick
100 g (3 ½ oz) honey
50 g (1 ¾ oz) unsalted butter
160 ml (⅔ cup) freshly squeezed lime juice
7 g (1 tsp) finely chopped chipotle chili in adobo sauce
Sea salt

A handful of fresh Thai basil (topping)

If you like crisp skin on your chicken, it needs to be dry from the very start. The trick is to leave the chicken, uncovered, in the refrigerator, overnight, so the skin can fully dry out. Flattened chicken is a ravishing and reliable way to get juicy meat, including the breast, as the juices circulate throughout the chicken, while the aromatic blend can be laid conveniently on top and won't slip off. Once you've squeezed all the juice out of the limes, arrange them on top of and underneath the chicken. This adds extra flavor, and looks really beautiful when served.

AROMATIC BLEND
Crush the loomi with the lower part of your palm or something heavy. Put the crushed loomi in an electric coffee grinder, along with the cinnamon, and grind to a fine powder. Put the powder in a small saucepan, add the honey, butter, lime juice, and chipotle chili; season with sea salt. Bring to a boil over high heat and boil for 1 minute then turn off the heat. Durability: 10 days refrigerated. Makes 240 ml (1 cup).

CHICKEN
Place the chicken, breast side down, on a cutting board and use a sharp, heavy knife or poultry shears to remove the backbone and neck; discard both. Turn the chicken over and press it flat. Rub the aromatic blend all over both sides of the chicken. Place the chicken, skin side up, in a roasting pan, add the reserved squeezed limes, if desired, and roast in a preheated 200°C (395°F) oven for 1 hour, or until tender, juicy, and crisp. The aromatic blend contains honey, so it may start to burn after 30–40 minutes. If this happens, lay a piece of parchment paper loosely on top of the chicken. Let the chicken rest for 5–10 minutes. Serve with plenty of Thai basil and the juices from the bottom of the pan.

SEASON: All year round
Main dish for 4

SEA SALT/JUNIPER/
LONG PEPPER/COCONUT
SUGAR/ ALLSPICE/
ROSEMARY

DUCK

FRIED AND MARINATED DUCK BREAST

2 duck breasts with skin (700 g / 25 oz)

CHARACTER
A refined, warm, and full-bodied blend with resoundingly beautiful resin notes.

VARIATIONS
The aromatic blend can also be used with beef, lamb, chicken, or game.

AROMATIC BLEND #20
30 (3 g) whole juniper berries
15 (2 g) whole allspice berries
2 (2 g) whole long pepper (see p. 279)
5 g (1 tbsp) coconut sugar
5 g (1 tbsp) finely chopped fresh rosemary
2 g (½ tsp) sea salt

This aromatic blend is one of my favorites. In fragrance and flavor, it's like taking a walk in a pine forest, with clouds of resin notes all around you. This dish is incredibly easy to make, but you'll need to start it the day before. Pre-frying and marinating the duck breasts means the aromatic blend gets absorbed by the meat itself, rather than just staying on the skin. Of course, you can also fry the duck breasts in one go, after marinating them for two hours at room temperature. But then you won't get the full pine forest experience! Cold duck slices (if you have any leftovers) also taste really good added to creamy salads. You can substitute 10 black peppercorns for the dried long pepper (these are small, thin, and oblong), if they are too hard to come by.

AROMATIC BLEND
Put the juniper berries, allspice berries, and long pepper in a mortar and pestle and grind to a medium-fine powder. Put the powder in a small bowl, add the coconut sugar, rosemary, and sea salt and stir to combine. Durability: Use immediately. Makes 50 ml (3 ¼ tbsp)

DUCK
DAY 1: Remove any membranes and dry the duck breasts on both sides. Cut the duck skin in a crisscross pattern with a sharp knife. Heat a medium frying pan over medium heat and fry the duck breasts, skin side down and without adding any fat to the pan or flipping the duck, for 3–5 minutes, or until golden and crisp. As fat accumulates in the pan, pour it off and reserve for the next day. Put the duck breasts, skin side up, in a glass or stainless steel roasting pan, rub the aromatic blend all over the meat, cover, and refrigerate overnight.

DAY 2: Remove the duck breasts from the refrigerator and let stand at room temperature for 2 hours. Heat a medium frying pan over medium-high heat and add all of the reserved duck fat. Fry the duck breasts, skin side up, for 3–4 minutes, or until dark golden. Turn the breasts over, so they are skin side down, and roast in a preheated 200°C (395°F) oven for 5–8 minutes, or until medium—the skin should be dark golden and crisp, but the meat should still be moist inside. Let rest for 5 minutes then cut into 2 cm (¾ in) thick slices and serve.

SEASON: All year round
Starter for 4–6

PAPRIKA / SPEARMINT / EGG / FENNEL SEED / CORIANDER SEED / RICE FLOUR / CUMIN / ONION / CEYLON CINNAMON

LAMB

GLAZED LAMB MEATBALLS

500 g (18 oz) ground lamb (not too lean)

CHARACTER
Warm, sweet, and highly aromatic, this exotic blend is full of flavors associated with the Middle East.

VARIATIONS
The aromatic blend can also be used with ground beef or pork, or added to meat dishes (without the eggs and rice flour). Alternatively, try using the blend in lasagna and vegetable or fish gratins.

AROMATIC BLEND #21
2.5 cm (1 in) (2 g) Ceylon cinnamon stick
2 g (1 tsp) whole fennel seeds
2 g (1 tsp) whole coriander seeds
2 g (1 tsp) whole cumin seeds
50 g (3½ tbsp) coarsely grated onion
10 g (2 tbsp) finely chopped fresh spearmint, plus more for topping
2 medium eggs
10 g (1 tbsp) rice flour
2 g (1 tsp) sweet paprika

Sea salt
60 ml (4 tbsp) pomegranate syrup (topping)

These meatballs smell and taste of the Middle East. If you can't get hold of pomegranate syrup, the dish will lack its fresh sweet tanginess, but you can cook the meatballs in a rustic tomato sauce instead. Adjust the herbs according to the season—fennel fronds, chives, oregano, tarragon, sorrel, and dill all work in this dish—and be sure to use them liberally.

AROMATIC BLEND
Put the cinnamon, along with the fennel, coriander, and cumin seeds, in an electric coffee grinder or mortar and pestle and grind to a fine powder. Put the powder in a small bowl, add the onion, finely chopped spearmint (10 g / 2 tbsp), eggs, rice flour, and sweet paprika and stir to combine. Durability: Use immediately. Makes 240 ml (1 cup).

MEATBALLS
Mix the ground lamb with a little sea salt in a large bowl then add the aromatic blend and stir thoroughly to combine. Use a 15 ml / 1 tbsp measuring spoon to divide the mixture into 30 meatballs (about 20 g or 4 tsp per ball) then use your hands to roll the meatballs into round, uniform balls. Put the meatballs on a parchment paper–lined baking sheet and roast in a preheated 220°C (420°F) oven for 8–10 minutes, or until golden but still juicy. Alternatively, fry the meatballs in a pan with a little cold-pressed olive oil for 5–8 minutes. Toss the meatballs with the pomegranate syrup and coarsely chopped spearmint leaves, and serve immediately.

SEASON: All year round
Main dish for 4
Makes 30 meatballs

ALLSPICE / GELATIN / SEA
SALT / CUBEB PEPPER /
BAY LEAVES / APPLE CIDER
VINEGAR / APPLE JUICE /
LONG PEPPER / CLOVES /
JUNIPER / WATER

PORK PRESERVED IN APPLE JELLY

680 g (1½ lb) piece boneless pork belly with skin

CHARACTER

A light and refined blend with fresh, sour flavor and mild notes of resin, apple, and pepper.

VARIATIONS

The aromatic blend can also be used with poultry, duck, or lamb. Adjust the cooking time accordingly.

AROMATIC BLEND #22

600 ml (2½ cups) cold water
200 ml (13 tbsp) unfiltered apple juice
200 ml (13 tbsp) unfiltered apple cider vinegar
4 (4 g) whole long pepper (see p. 279)
15 (0.8 g) whole cubeb pepper berries (see p. 278)
4 g (1 tsp) sea salt
8 (1.6 g) whole allspice berries
4 (0.8 g) whole cloves
8 (0.8 g) whole juniper berries
4 (2 g) fresh bay leaves
5 leaves gelatin

Tender, juicy pork in fresh, golden apple jelly makes for an unexpected treat. Enjoy the meat, its fat, and the apple jelly, on toasted rye or sourdough bread with mustard and mild pickles. The fat contains most of the aroma, so it tastes incredibly good spread on warm toast and allowed to melt. You can shred the meat and use it in salads, or on top of root vegetable purées or soups. Using a pressure cooker allows the meat to acquire more flavor, and cuts the cooking time in half. Cubeb pepper berries and whole long pepper (these are small, thin, and oblong) are dried whole spices that deliver deep, warm, and ravishingly sweet resin notes, but if it requires too much detective work to find them, simply substitute both with 15 whole black peppercorns instead. The pork tastes best after 3 to 4 days, so plan ahead and allow plenty of time to let it preserve in the fridge; it keeps well for up to a month.

AROMATIC BLEND

Combine all the ingredients (except the gelatin) in a large bowl. Durability: Use the same day. Makes 600 ml (2½ cups).

PORK

Day 1: Cut the skin off the pork belly and discard. Divide the meat into 3 pieces and place in the pressure cooker, along with the aromatic blend (the gelatin is added later). Put on the lid and turn up the heat. When the pressure cooker makes 'noise' and sputters with steam, turn down the heat, but make sure there is still plenty of steam coming out of the valve. Cook the pork for 30 minutes then turn off the heat and let stand for at least 30 minutes. The waiting time is important to the taste, so be patient.

Soak the gelatin leaves in cold water for 5 minutes. Remove the meat from the pressure cooker, cut it into small pieces, and put it in a clean (1 l/4 cup) preserves jar or container.

Meanwhile, reduce the liquid that's left in the pressure cooker, uncovered and over high heat, to 600 ml (2½ cups) then turn off the heat, so it doesn't boil. Take the soaked gelatin leaves out of the water, add to the pressure cooker, and whisk until completely dissolved. Pour the warm, reduced aromatic blend, including the whole spices, which are still giving off flavor, over the pork, seal the jar, and refrigerate at least overnight and preferably 3–4 days.

Alternatively, the pork can be cooked over low heat in a covered pot on the stove for 1–1½ hours, or until tender. If the liquid evaporates too quickly, gradually add a little water. Allow the meat to stand for at least 30 minutes, and follow the above procedure for finishing the pork.

Day 2: To serve, simply shred the meat with a fork or cut it into thick slices. If you leave the fat on and use it on warm toast, or to top soups, it will melt and add more flavour.

SEASON: All year round
Starter or side dish for 4–6

BLACK PEPPERCORN/SEA SALT/SMOKED PAPRIKA/ BAY LEAF/CANE SUGAR/ FENUGREEK/ALLSPICE

BEEF

JUICY BRAISED BEEF BRISKET

2 kg (4 ½ lb) boneless beef brisket

CHARACTER

A harmonious, rich, addictive blend with a refined flavor profile, subtle sweetness, and mild smoky notes.

VARIATIONS

The aromatic blend can also be used with pork, poultry, duck, and lamb. Adjust the cooking and marinating times accordingly.

AROMATIC BLEND #23

1 l (4 cups) water
455 g (1 lb) light cane sugar
150 g (5 ¼ oz) sea salt
6 (3 g) fresh bay leaves
16 g (2 tbsp) whole black peppercorns
10 g (2 tsp) whole fenugreek seeds
10 (2 g) whole allspice berries
8 g (4 tsp) sweet smoked paprika

1.5 l (6 cups) cold water, for boiling
Fresh herbs (topping)

In the Balkan countries, you see many versions of wind-dried beef seasoned with, for example, garlic, cumin, fenugreek, and paprika. All of them are strongly influenced by the now-famous specialty, pastrami (brined, smoked, and braised brisket). My aromatic blend is inspired by this specialty, but I have left out the wind drying and smoking, as well as the thick layer of crushed spices that are rubbed around the meat before it is smoked and then braised until tender. My aromatic blend is simple, and the result is still an exceptionally tasty and juicy piece of meat. The brisket can be served hot in the stock, perhaps with boiled potatoes and root vegetables, or used on rye bread, in sandwiches, or as a topping for lentil and bean soups.

AROMATIC BLEND

Put all the aromatic blend ingredients in a medium saucepan and bring to a boil. Reduce the heat and simmer, covered, for 10 minutes then let cool to room temperature. Durability: 2–3 weeks refrigerated. Makes 1.2 l (5 cups).

BEEF

DAY 1: Prick the brisket with a thick needle or fork then place in a deep roasting pan large enough to hold it snugly. Pour the aromatic blend (room temperature) over the meat then place a clean cloth on top. This will draw the juices upward and prevent the top of the meat from drying out. Marinate the brisket for 36 hours in the refrigerator.

DAY 2: Take the brisket out of the marinade (the aromatic blend) and rinse it thoroughly. (You can use the marinade one more time to marinate beef; store it in the refrigerator until ready to use). Put the brisket in a pressure cooker with the cold water then put on the lid and turn up the heat. When

the pressure cooker makes 'noise' and sputters with steam, turn down the heat slightly, but make sure there is still plenty of steam coming out of the valve. Cook the brisket for 1 hour then turn off the heat, and let stand for at least 30 minutes. The waiting time is important to the taste, so be patient.

Cut the brisket into slices then pour the hot stock (the liquid from the pressure cooker) over it, sprinkle with the fresh herbs, and serve. If not serving immediately, store the brisket, in the stock, in the refrigerator.

Alternatively, the beef can be cooked over low heat in a covered pot on the stove for 2–2½ hours, or until tender (using the same amount of water). Let the meat stand for at least 30 minutes, and follow the procedure above for serving.

SEASON: All year round.
Main dish for 4–6

SEASONS OF PLENTY

Cooking according to the seasons is a highly aromatic and healthy way to eat. It's also often about finally being able to experience a taste or texture that you've been longing for and missed for a terribly long time. Some people cook this way for the simple pleasure of putting their fork in the very first new potatoes. For others, cooking by the seasons is just common sense. It is, after all, the healthiest way to eat. For me, it comes down to the fact that seasonal ingredients possess the greatest amount of aromatic substances.

A few years ago, I planted a fig tree in my cold greenhouse. I love that tree, because I can pluck a ripe fig effortlessly, and go on a fleeting trip back in time to the Greek archipelago, and the days of my youth. The fig is always plump and there are only a few light stripes visible on its supple, deep-purple skin. Still warm from the sun, the fig has a baby-soft texture, and is full of cooling, piquant aromas and juicy sweetness. Because it's been allowed to ripen on the tree, the fig's aromatic substances are wide awake and harmonize beautifully with its natural sweetness. That is precisely what I fall in love with and miss when it's not there. It's a sensory experience that's absent of any handling, packaging, or storage. It can be enjoyed in the moment, and will hopefully lead, as it does at my house, to pure gluttony, because it doesn't get much better than that.

Freshness is the result of the unique balance of flavor, texture, and sweetness that arises when certain ingredients come into season and fully ripen. When fruits and vegetables are ripe, they release the greatest amount of aromatic substances, and achieve their fullest expression of fragrance and taste. This makes it easy to know when fruit is ready to eat. It's different with vegetables, which are often assessed in terms of their size, texture, and appearance, because their characteristic fragrances cannot be perceived until they're opened up, peeled, or cut into pieces.

When an ingredient is fully ripe, it acquires its true personality and character. This is because the most interesting fragrances and flavors are not established until the very end of the ripening process. Picking unripe fruits and vegetables, with a view to cold storage and after-ripening, inevitably leads to disappointment, as their full aromatic potential has yet to be achieved. Most fruits and vegetables are dominated by sweet and sour aromatic substances. With ripening, comes sweetness, and the riper that fruits and vegetables are allowed to become, the more sweetness they contain. This concentration of sweetness is overwhelming and very elegant, as it is distinct and natural. Sweetness is always relevant, because it amplifies the overall taste of food, and when an ingredient is inherently sweet, additional sweetening isn't required. And if any sweetness does need to be added, it can be in smaller amounts.

IF YOU GROW YOUR OWN FRUITS AND VEGETABLES, YOU CAN EASILY BECOME ADDICTED, BECAUSE THEY MAKE YOU SO HAPPY

When fruits and vegetable are fresh and newly harvested, they have the most interesting texture. There is a loud crunching sound and a corresponding feeling in your wrist, as you tear kale and spinach leaves, or curl them together. Something similar happens when you stick your knife into the first new potatoes, and meet resistance from the moist and sticky starch. But preparing fresh, newly harvested fruits and vegetables is also a quick and healthy way to eat, simply because they require less cooking. The skin is still porous and thin, and only needs to be rinsed or gently brushed, and the short preparation time means the taste will be more fully experienced and the nutrients better utilized. If fruits and vegetables are allowed to grow until they're big and heavy, before being harvested and stored, they need to be cooked far longer, which in turn means a greater loss of aromas and valuable nutrients.

For me, freshness is a distinct taste that contains amazing vitality. If you grow your own fruits and vegetables, you can easily become addicted, because they make you so happy. There is just something about the fragrance and flavor notes, the sound, the sweetness, the temperature, and the beautiful texture of fresh ingredients. It's hard to define. Maybe it's that all these factors come together to create unusually high levels of aesthetics and aromatics that many people have never experienced, or perhaps have long forgotten. The goal of the food industry is durability. When you enter a supermarket, there are

FRESHNESS IS A DISTINCT TASTE THAT CONTAINS AMAZING VITALITY

very few ingredients you can't obtain year round. Maintaining this range means the fruits and vegetables must be picked before they're ripe, and transported across borders, often from very far away. In order for these ingredients to arrive fresh at your supermarket, they're usually kept in cold storage and slowly ripened from the time they're harvested. They may sit like that for months, and the longer fruits and vegetables are stored, the more nutrients and flavors are lost. This makes my point quite clear: Cooking seasonal, preferably organic and biodynamic, produce from your local region, purchased straight from the growers, whether at a good store or your local farmers' market, is the healthiest, smartest, and tastiest way to cook.

SUMMER
VEGE-
TABLES

LEMON VERBENA/SEA SALT/BROWN MUSTARD SEED/CREAM/SUMAC/TARRAGON

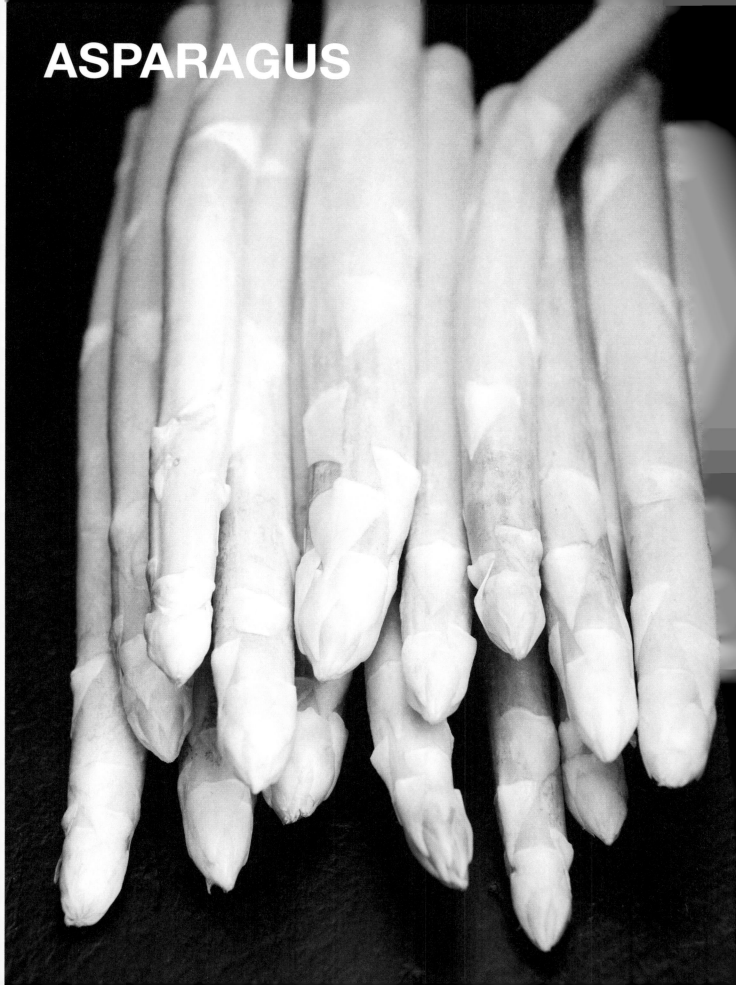

ASPARAGUS

BOILED ASPARAGUS

500 g (18 oz) white or green asparagus

CHARACTER

A creamy, crunchy, and nutty blend with subtle notes of citrus and anise.

VARIATIONS

The aromatic blend can also be served hot, warm, or cold, with cooked or steamed vegetables, potatoes, fish, or shellfish.

AROMATIC BLEND #24

20 g (2 tbsp) whole brown mustard seeds
200 ml (13 tbsp) heavy cream
5 g (1 tbsp) finely chopped fresh tarragon, plus more for topping
5 g (1 tbsp) finely chopped fresh lemon verbena
4 g (2 tsp) sumac, plus more for topping (see p. 279)
Sea salt

Brown mustard seeds are slightly bitter with a strong and burning taste. But, if the seeds are dry-roasted for about 15 seconds in a very hot, dry pan until they 'jump' and change color to gray, the heat will soothe the strong taste, and make the seeds mild and nutty. Sumac is another favorite in my kitchen. The dried, rust-red seeds of a fruit that is native to the Mediterranean, sumac is often available as a moist red powder. The taste is acidic, with a pronounced fruitiness that is less tart than lemon or vinegar. Sumac has the great advantage of not being a messy liquid, but a dry red powder that can be sprinkled over all sorts of dishes to give them an elegant sharpness.

AROMATIC BLEND

Heat a small saucepan over high heat. Add the mustard seeds and dry-roast for 5–15 seconds, or until they 'jump' and turn gray in color. Add the cream (it will sputter and bubble due to the strong heat), and continue boiling until creamy and reduced to 160 ml (⅔ cup). Add the tarragon, lemon verbena, and sumac, season with sea salt, and continue boiling for 1 minute then turn off the heat. If the aromatic blend becomes too thick, whisk in a little water. Cover and keep hot. Durability: Use immediately. Makes 160 ml (⅔ cup).

ASPARAGUS

Take a careful, firm hold of the tip and peel down to the root of the asparagus with a vegetable peeler. Snap off the woody ends. Boil the asparagus in salted water for 5–8 minutes, or until tender. Pour the hot aromatic blend over the asparagus, and top with more sumac and tarragon.

SEASON; May–July
Starter or side dish for 4

ALMONDS / SEA SALT / BUTTER / LEMON / BITTER ALMOND / FENUGREEK / GINGER ROOT / PARSLEY / BLACK PEPPERCORN

BEAN

GRILLED BEANS

500 g (18 oz) purple or green beans

CHARACTER

A refined, pure, distinctive almond-flavored blend with subtle herbal notes and a fine sharpness.

VARIATIONS

The aromatic blend can also be used as the fat to fry in, or as a warm sauce to be poured over vegetables, meat, poultry, or fish. You can top boiled potatoes or steaks with it, as an alternative to cold butter, or spread it on bread or toast, or in sandwiches.

AROMATIC BLEND #25

1 g (¼ tsp) whole fenugreek seeds
100 g (3 ½ oz) soft unsalted butter
25 g (5 tsp) finely chopped almonds
10 g (2 tsp) finely chopped fresh flat-leaf parsley
10 g (¾ tbsp) finely grated fresh ginger with peel
3 g (½ tbsp) finely grated lemon zest
2 g (½ tsp) sea salt
½ (0.5 g) finely grated bitter almond (optional) (see p. 277)
A pinch of freshly ground black pepper

Beans are extremely suitable for quick grilling at a high temperature. Choose plump, thick beans, so that they will be juicy but still crunchy when served. They can, of course, be fried directly in the aromatic blend, but the smoky flavor from the grill works wonders. I have tried making the aromatic blend in a food processor, but the results are actually much better, in terms of both taste and appearance, when all the ingredients are chopped and grated by hand.

AROMATIC BLEND

Heat a small frying pan over high heat. Add the fenugreek seeds and dry-roast for 5–15 seconds, or until fragrant and beginning to take on color. Immediately put the fenugreek in an electric coffee grinder or a mortar and pestle and to grind to a fine powder. Put the powder in a small bowl then add the butter, almonds, parsley, ginger, lemon zest, sea salt, and bitter almond, if using; season with freshly ground black pepper. Stir until fully combined, cover, and refrigerate until ready to use. Durability: 5 days refrigerated. Makes 150 g (5 ¼ oz).

BEANS

Preheat a grill to hot. Pinch off the ends of the beans and grill, without oil, for 3–4 minutes, or until tender but with a little bite. When serving, use 70–100 g (2 ½–3 ½ oz) of the aromatic blend for every 500 g (18 oz) of beans. Heat the aromatic blend in a small saucepan over medium-high heat just until the butter melts then pour it over the grilled beans and serve. Reserve the remaining aromatic blend for later use.

SEASON: August–September
Starter or side dish for 4

BARBERRY BERRIES/SEA SALT FLAKES/SPEARMINT/ CASHEW NUT BUTTER

CUCUMBER

JUICY AND CREAMY CUCUMBER SALAD

1½ cucumbers (455 g / 1 lb)

CHARACTER
A mild, soft, refreshing, pure, and elegant blend with nutty and minty notes.

VARIATIONS
The aromatic blend can also be used with raw apples, pears, fennel, tomatoes, mangoes, radishes, apricots, and juicy lettuce leaves.

AROMATIC BLEND #26
4 g (1 tsp) sea salt flakes
60 g (3 tbsp) cashew nut butter, room temperature
15 g (3 tbsp) sun-dried barberry berries
10 g (⅓ oz) fresh spearmint

This salad is cooling, creamy, and juicy, and makes an ideal accompaniment to grilled fish, seafood, meat, or poultry on a hot summer day. If you add slices of boiled new potatoes, this can be a main course. Barberry berries are small ruby-red berries that resemble raisins. They typically have a tart, piquant flavor, but can vary greatly in taste. Some barberry berries, especially the Iranian ones, will send you straight to heaven—they can be as addictive as candy—others you'd rather forget. The spearmint can be replaced by dill, tarragon, or basil.

AROMATIC BLEND
Measure the amounts of all the ingredients in separate bowls and set aside. Durability: Use immediately Makes 100 ml (7 tbsp).

CUCUMBER
Cut the cucumbers into paper-thin strips / slices with a mandoline slicer or very sharp knife. Put the cucumbers in a medium bowl, sprinkle with the sea salt flakes, and let stand for 10 minutes, or until the cucumbers turn soft and there's a little cucumber water in the bottom of the bowl. Add the rest of the aromatic blend ingredients and use your hands to massage them into the cucumbers until the cashew nut butter is completely dissolved and the salad has a creamy appearance. Use some force while doing this, so the spearmint releases its aroma.

SEASON: April–October
Starter or side dish for 4

BUTTERMILK/CHICKPEA FLOUR/ANISE SEED/ NIGELLA/FENNEL SEED/ CUMIN

FENNEL

DEEP-FRIED FENNEL FRITTERS

1 fennel bulb (350 g / 12 ¼ oz)

CHARACTER

This blend reminds me of delicate falafel, crisp and featherlight, with lots of roasted nutty notes, tanginess, and a touch of warming anise.

VARIATIONS

The aromatic blend can also be used with thinly sliced vegetables, fish, or shellfish.

AROMATIC BLEND #27

300 g (1 ¼ cups) finely ground chickpea flour
4 g (2 tsp) whole nigella seeds
3 g (1½ tsp) whole fennel seeds
3 g (1½ tsp) whole cumin seeds
2 g (1 tsp) whole anise seeds
300 ml (1 ¼ cups) buttermilk, plus more as needed

1.5 l (6 cups) cold-pressed neutral oil, such as canola or peanut oil, for deep-frying
Sea salt flakes
Lemon slices (topping)

You can never have too many delicate vegetable fritters. Chickpea flour tastes sweet and faintly nutty and it seems lighter than if you use wheat flour for the fritter coating. Get your hands on chickpea flour that is very finely ground—this will ensure a thick, perfectly crisp coating. As you're dipping the fennel in the chickpea flour and buttermilk, some lumps may arise, but it doesn't matter—they'll crisp up during the deep-frying.

AROMATIC BLEND

In a wide, shallow dish, combine the chickpea flour with the nigella, fennel, cumin, and anise seeds. Pour the buttermilk into a second wide, shallow dish. Durability: Use the same day. Makes 300 g (10 ½ oz)

FENNEL

Peel the fennel and cut the bulb in half then cut the halves lengthwise into slices that are 1–1.5 cm (⅜–⅝ in) thick. Using tongs, turn the fennel slices in the chickpea flour, making sure they are completely coated and shaking off any excess flour, then dip them in the buttermilk. Repeat this process, dipping the fennel in chickpea flour then buttermilk then chickpea flour, until the fennel pieces are thickly covered (the last layer should be chickpea flour).

Put the slices on a parchment paper–lined baking sheet, and set aside until ready to fry.

Heat the cold-pressed neutral oil in a wok to 180°C (360°F). Working in batches, fry the fennel slices for 3–5 minutes, or until golden brown and crisp. Place the fennel slices on a rack and serve piping hot, seasoned with sea salt flakes and lemon slices.

If the frying oil is kept under 200°C (395°F) it can be reused several times. Cool the oil slightly then pour it through a coffee filter or fine-mesh sieve. Keep the oil in a clean jar, cool and dry, until the next time you need it.

SEASON: June–October
Snack for 2

CINNAMON LEAVES / OLIVE OIL / CHILI / MACE / BLACK PEPPER / BERGAMOT / SEA SALT / CORIANDER SEED / GARLIC

LEEK

SILKY FRAGRANT LEEKS

1 kg (2 ¼ lb) leeks

CHARACTER

An ultra-tart, fresh, pure, mild blend, with a creamy texture.

VARIATIONS

The aromatic blend can also be used to cook other vegetables, such as bok choy, pak choy, cabbage, spinach, green beans, carrots, or parsley roots.

AROMATIC BLEND #28

0.5 g (¼ tsp) whole coriander seeds
0.3 g (⅛ tsp) whole mace or nutmeg
2 (10 g) cloves garlic, thinly sliced
8–10 (3 g) whole dried cinnamon leaves (see p. 278)
A pinch of chili flakes
5 g (¾ tbsp) finely grated bergamot or lemon zest
45 ml (3 tbsp) freshly squeezed bergamot or lemon juice
45 ml (3 tbsp) cold-pressed olive oil
150 ml (10 tbsp) boiling water
Sea salt
Freshly ground black pepper

175 g (6 ¼ oz) crumbled feta (topping)

The aromatic blend in this recipe first acts as the cooking liquid and later becomes a creamy sauce, thereby ensuring that no flavor or nutrients are lost. Cinnamon leaves can be hard to find, but are an experience you should not miss. They lend something light, sweet, and perfumed to the leeks—it's more of a scent than a taste—and emit the most ravishing clouds of aroma every time you lift the pot lid. You can replace the bergamot with ordinary lemon. Or try using orange, which will make the dish sweeter and less tart.

AROMATIC BLEND

Put the coriander seeds and mace in an electric coffee grinder or mortar and pestle and grind to a fine powder. Put the powder in a medium bowl then add the garlic, cinnamon leaves, and chili flakes. Add the bergamot zest and juice, cold-pressed olive oil, and boiling water then season with sea salt and freshly ground black pepper. Durability: Use the same day. Makes 240 ml (1 cup).

LEEKS

Cut the dark and pale green tops off the leeks and remove the 2 outermost layers. Trim the roots, leaving them intact as much as possible, then cut the leeks into 10 cm (4 in) long pieces (the cleaned weight should be approx. 500 g / 18 oz). Thoroughly but gently rinse the leeks in water.

Put the aromatic blend in a medium sauté pan and arrange the leeks, in a closely packed single layer, on top—the aromatic blend should almost cover the leeks. Bring to a boil then reduce the heat to low and simmer, covered, for about 25 minutes, or until a sharp knife can go all the way through the leeks without any resistance. Remove the leeks from the sauté pan and keep warm. Continue simmering the aromatic blend until reduced to a thick sauce. If it boils down too quickly and begins to dry out, gradually add a little cold water. Toss the warm leeks in the reduced sauce, top with the crumbled feta, and serve.

SEASON: August–April
Starter or side dish for 4

OREGANO/LEMON JUICE/ SUMAC/SEA SALT FLAKES

ONION

GRILLED ONION SALAD

500 g (18 oz) young onions with green tops

CHARACTER
Light, fresh, and crisp, this blend is quiet but full of pure flavor; it's slightly creamy and has subtle notes of fruit.

VARIATIONS
The aromatic blend can also be used on top of fish, ripe fruit, or other grilled vegetables.

AROMATIC BLEND #29
45 ml (3 tbsp) freshly squeezed lemon juice
30 g (1 oz) fresh oregano
4 g (2 tsp) sumac (see p. 279)
Sea salt flakes

Cold-pressed olive oil, for grilling

Za'atar is a traditional Arab salad made with raw red onion, lemon juice, wild broadleaf thyme (also called za'atar; it looks a lot like oregano), and sumac. The same word is also used for a beautiful dried spice mixture consisting of sumac, sesame seeds, thyme, and salt. I tasted both when I was in Palestine, but it was the fresh salad combination that left the strongest impression on me. There's no oil used in the salad, and the acidity of the lemon juice "cooks" the thyme leaves, rendering them soft, succulent, and incredibly tasty. In my version, I've swapped the raw red onion for grilled young onions to add some crunchy, juicy texture, plus extra sweetness and smokiness, and I've used oregano instead of thyme. Young onions are onions that are pulled out of the ground early and still have their green tops attached. Unlike scallions or green onions, young onions have a small bulb at the bottom. They can be replaced with 400 g (14 oz) regular yellow onions (choose small ones), which are available year round, and need a little longer on the grill. You can also add figs, pears, melons, or creamy feta to turn this salad into a meal. The aromatic blend should be made at the very last minute; otherwise, it will turn limp and dull.

AROMATIC BLEND
Put the lemon juice, oregano, and sumac in a small bowl, season with sea salt flakes, and toss to combine. Let stand for 10 minutes. Durability: Use immediately. Makes 400 ml (1 ⅔ cups).

ONIONS
Preheat a grill to hot. Remove the green tops of the onions (discard or use them in soups) then cut in half lengthwise, leaving the roots intact to hold the onions together. Brush the onions with a little cold-pressed olive oil and grill, turning once, for 10–15 minutes per side, or until they begin to release a little moisture but are still crunchy—the onions should not be falling apart. Divide the onions into individual layers and roughly chop. Serve hot, topped with the aromatic blend.

SEASON: June–August
Starter or side dish for 4

FENNEL SEED/NIGELLA/ CUMIN/BROWN MUSTARD SEED/FENUGREEK

ZUCCHINI

ROASTED ZUCCHINI SALAD

800 g (1 ¾ lb) zucchini

CHARACTER

A harmonious, piquant, deep, and unusual blend; it has subtle bitterness and refined, warm nutty notes.

VARIATIONS

The aromatic blend (without the topping) can also be used with pasta, salads, legumes, vegetables, fish, or meat, as well as sprinkled on sandwiches, flatbread, or soup.

AROMATIC BLEND #30

4 g (½ tbsp) whole nigella seeds
3.5 g (½ tbsp) whole cumin seeds
3 g (¼ tbsp) whole fenugreek seeds
2.5 g (½ tbsp) whole fennel seeds
5 g (½ tbsp) whole brown mustard seeds

Sea salt
30 ml (2 tbsp) unfiltered apple cider vinegar (topping)
30 ml (2 tbsp) cold-pressed olive oil (topping)
40 g (1 ⅖ oz) freshly shaved Parmesan cheese (topping)
Fresh bronze fennel flower umbels (optional; topping)

If served cold, the zucchini tastes almost as though pickled, so it's excellent for enjoying as leftovers the next day. You can naturally add crunchy, sweet romaine leaves to give this juicy salad more heft. The bronze fennel flower umbels can be replaced by your favorite fresh herbs, or left out completely. The aromatic blend is inspired by *panch phoron*, a classic Indian spice mix, consisting of equal parts fennel, cumin, nigella, fenugreek, and mustard seeds. It's used to flavor vegetable and legume-based dishes, and produces a pleasant interplay of tastes, as the spices are not ground but added whole. In my version, the spices are roasted and ground, which creates a more harmonious flavor that's warm, deep, and nutty. It's a subtle flavoring, but you could easily become addicted to it, because even a small sprinkling will make all sorts of dishes a bit more interesting.

AROMATIC BLEND

Heat a small frying pan over high heat. Add the nigella, cumin, fenugreek, and fennel seeds and dry-roast for 5–15 seconds, or until fragrant and beginning to take on color. Immediately pour the seeds onto a plate to prevent them from burning. Put the pan back over high heat, add the mustard seeds and dry-roast for 5–15 seconds, or until they begin to 'jump' and turn gray in color. Put all the spices in an electric coffee grinder and grind to a fine powder. Durability: 2 weeks at room temperature. Makes: 18 g (2 ¼ tbsp).

ZUCCHINI

Trim the zucchini then cut crosswise into ½ cm (⅛ in) thick slices. Arrange the zucchini, in a single layer, on 3 parchment paper–lined roasting pans. Sprinkle with half the aromatic blend and season with sea salt. Roast in a preheated 230°C (450°F) oven for 20 minutes, or until the zucchini is almost translucent but hasn't developed any color yet. Remove the zucchini from the oven, drizzle with the apple cider vinegar and cold-pressed olive oil, and let stand for 5 minutes. Serve the salad hot or cold, topped with the shaved Parmesan, fresh bronze fennel flower umbels, if using, and a little more of the aromatic blend. Reserve the remaining aromatic blend for another use.

SEASON: July–October
Starter or side dish for 4

COCONUT SUGAR/CHIVE BLOSSOM/SPEARMINT/ BACON

RADISH

RADISH SALAD

300 g (10 ½ oz) cleaned radishes without green tops

CHARACTER

A juicy, smoky, and full-bodied blend, with delicate onion notes, a hint of menthol, and elegant caramelization.

VARIATIONS

The aromatic blend can also be used with thinly sliced raw apple, pear, fennel, cucumbers, or tomatoes, as well as with potatoes, salads, or soup.

AROMATIC BLEND #31

150 g (5 ¼ oz) whole bacon slices
15 g (2 ½ tbsp) chive blossoms
10 g (2 tbsp) finely chopped fresh spearmint
10 g (1 tbsp) coconut sugar

100 g (3 ½ oz) crumbled feta (topping)

When it comes to aromatic potential, bacon grease combined with fresh herbs and dried spices is a perfect match, because the fat encapsulates the aromas and holds them firmly. In this dish, the mint flavor is further amplified if the bacon is enjoyed cold. Chives bloom in May, but just before that happens, they have delicate, lilac-brown buds filled with delightfully gentle and refined onion notes. Almost any herbs and flowers can be used in this aromatic blend—just make sure the coconut sugar is the last thing you sprinkle on top, so that it lies across the herbs and protects them from the high heat.

AROMATIC BLEND

Put the bacon on a baking sheet and sprinkle with the chive blossoms and spearmint, followed by the coconut sugar. Roast in a preheated 220°C (420°F) oven for 15–20 minutes, or until the bacon is golden brown and crisp. Durability: Use immediately. Makes 240 ml (1 cup).

RADISHES

Cut the radishes into paper-thin slices and put in a medium bowl. Add the feta and let stand at least 15 minutes. Top the radish salad with the hot aromatic blend, and serve.

SEASON: April–September
Starter or side dish for 4

TURMERIC ROOT/CUMIN/
NIGELLA/BUTTER/SEA
SALT/FENNEL SEED/BAY
LEAVES/CHILI FLAKES/
MAPLE SYRUP/BROWN
MUSTARD SEED

TOMATO

TOMATO SALAD

800 g (1 ¾ lb) ripe tomatoes

CHARACTER

An elegant, warm, and mild blend that's also exotic, unusual, and highly addictive; incredibly fragrant and piquant.

VARIATIONS

The aromatic blend can also be used with other raw and cooked vegetables or as a dressing with crunchy, juicy salad leaves, as well as in fruit and vegetable chutneys. It's particularly excellent with broiled or baked fish, poultry, or root vegetables.

AROMATIC BLEND #32

2.4 g (1 tsp) whole nigella seeds
2.4 g (1 tsp) whole cumin seeds
1.7 g (1 tsp) whole fennel seeds
3.7 g (1 tsp) whole brown mustard seeds
30 g (1 oz) unsalted butter
25 g (5 tsp) maple syrup or golden syrup
1.5 g (½ tsp) finely grated fresh turmeric with peel
2 (1 g) fresh bay leaves, finely-chopped (see p. 277)
A pinch of chili flakes
Sea salt

200 g (7 oz) piece feta (topping)
90 g (3 ¼ oz) thinly sliced onion rings (topping)

This salad is classic yet not. If your tomatoes lack sweetness and sunshine, this aromatic blend provides a simple and elegant remedy. It turns everything upside down. Though not strong, it's highly sophisticated. This blend is best when warm, so if you make it ahead, be sure to warm it before using. And when young onions (see p. 167) come into season in late July, they are ideal to use alongside the tomatoes.

AROMATIC BLEND

Heat a small frying pan over high heat. Add the nigella, cumin, and fennel seeds and dry-roast for 5–15 seconds, or until fragrant and beginning to take on color. Immediately pour the seeds onto a plate to prevent them from burning. Put the pan back over high heat, add the mustard seeds, and dry-roast for 5–15 seconds, or until they begin to 'jump' and turn gray in color. Put all the spices in an electric coffee grinder and grind to a fine powder. Put the powder, along with the butter, maple syrup, turmeric, bay leaves, and chili flakes in a small saucepan, season with sea salt, and bring to a boil. Continue boiling for 30 seconds then turn off the heat. Keep warm. Durability: 4 days at room temperature. Makes 60 ml (4 tbsp).

TOMATOES

Cut the tomatoes into thick chunks or wedges, and arrange on a plate. Divide the feta into 4 large chunks and add to the tomatoes. Top with the thinly sliced onion, drizzle with the warm aromatic blend, and serve at once.

SEASON: June–September
Starter for 4

ADVENTURES IN MY SWEDISH COUNTRY GARDEN

Sixteen years ago, I moved out of Copenhagen, and acquired my first garden, on a peninsula in the middle of a Danish nature reserve. Ever since that day, I've felt the need to get out and work in the garden. It affects me on many levels, and has many different functions, depending entirely on how I feel.

If I wake up in the morning and have any unease, I go straight to the garden. I drop everything, pull on my boots, and spend eight hours working the soil with my hands, moving rocks, and getting bruises. The next morning, I can catch up on my neglected work with peace of mind. I rarely sit and relax in my garden—I thrive best when I'm doing something. Compared to my work, the garden is a simple affair. I relax by weeding, digging the soil, pruning the trees, and making sure that all the plants are doing well. In the garden, my everyday frustrations are replaced with calm and confidence. I feel grounded and I can be myself. It's also where, strangely enough, I make the important decisions for my work. The pieces fall naturally into place when I'm in the garden. That's how it's always been.

Today, I live in the countryside of southern Sweden, surrounded by nature that is protected by UNESCO. This is where I keep my atelier: a professional kitchen and an office, plus a cold greenhouse, which is an extension of the atelier. Over the past eight years, I have tried to create a garden that does not feel like a ball and chain or a theatre stage, but a source of inspiration that makes me better at everything I spend my time on. It's a kind of cloister garden, minus the convent, the nuns, and the high protective walls, but full of rare herbs and medicinal plants, plus berries, several types of cabbage, and other fruits and vegetables, especially old heirloom varieties.

Plants interest me more than anything else. They make demands and ask questions of me—not vice versa. The garden is a combination of wildness, chemistry, and aesthetics. It's where I can experience aromatic compounds in their completely naked state, and see beauty that has not yet been disturbed by handling or processing. I can't quite explain what it is. I can only say how it feels. This is the place I most like being and where everything feels right. The atmosphere is quiet and not at all hectic. There's no noise, but it is still dramatically intense and emotional, with aromas that are raw and unmixed, and in such quantities that you can almost swim in them.

I'm greedy when it comes to scent and flavor, and in the greenhouse and surrounding garden, I have a chance to be satiated. There are exotic and mysterious plants, handpicked from all over the world, and every day is like standing in a perfume laboratory, because the top notes are so concentrated. At their peak, when the aromas are almost too much, I sometimes get dizzy and will even feel a headache coming on.

IT'S ALWAYS THE SAME—THE BALANCE BETWEEN A PLANT'S ARROGANCE AND HUMILITY, WHICH TEASES YOU AGAIN AND AGAIN, OR SWEEPS YOU OFF YOUR FEET

It's always the same—the balance between a plant's arrogance and humility, which teases you again and again, or sweeps you off your feet. Take, for example, Israeli Habek mint (*Mentha longifolia 'Habek'*), which grows quickly, and now dominates the bottom of my greenhouse. When the leaves are relatively young, they contain balsamic sweetness, warm spearmint, and a hint of citrus and sage. Later in the season, the long, narrow leaves acquire considerable bitterness and a heavy dominance that prevents the more delicate notes from breaking through. As soon as the plant is pruned back, however, the balance returns to its leaves.

My latest plant purchase is the epitome of humility. Andean sage (*Salvia discolor*) is excellent for brewing tea, as well as for flavoring lemonade or ice cream. If you put the big silvery leaves and flowers into boiling water, notes of black currant and eucalyptus are released first, followed by mint and lavender, and finally green apple. The lovely purple-black flowers are a whole story on their own. They're full of creamy nectar, which is juicy and tastes honey-sweet, with faint acidity and complex fragrance notes that would put violets (*Viola odorata*) and roses (*Rosa damascena, Rosa rugosa, Rosa centifolia*) to shame. Not a day goes by in the kitchen when I don't subject the roots, lea-

THE GARDEN IS A COMBINATION OF WILDNESS, CHEMISTRY, AND AESTHETICS

ves, seeds, and flowers to all kinds of preparation methods and combinations, hoping to find the sweet spot—the point where the maximum number of interesting aromatic compounds are released, and can be maintained for as long as possible. That is primordial power. And you can't help but react, because it affects you enormously. You turn off the everyday trivialities and just enjoy. For a moment, you forget all your worries. Aromas leave no trace, only memories ...

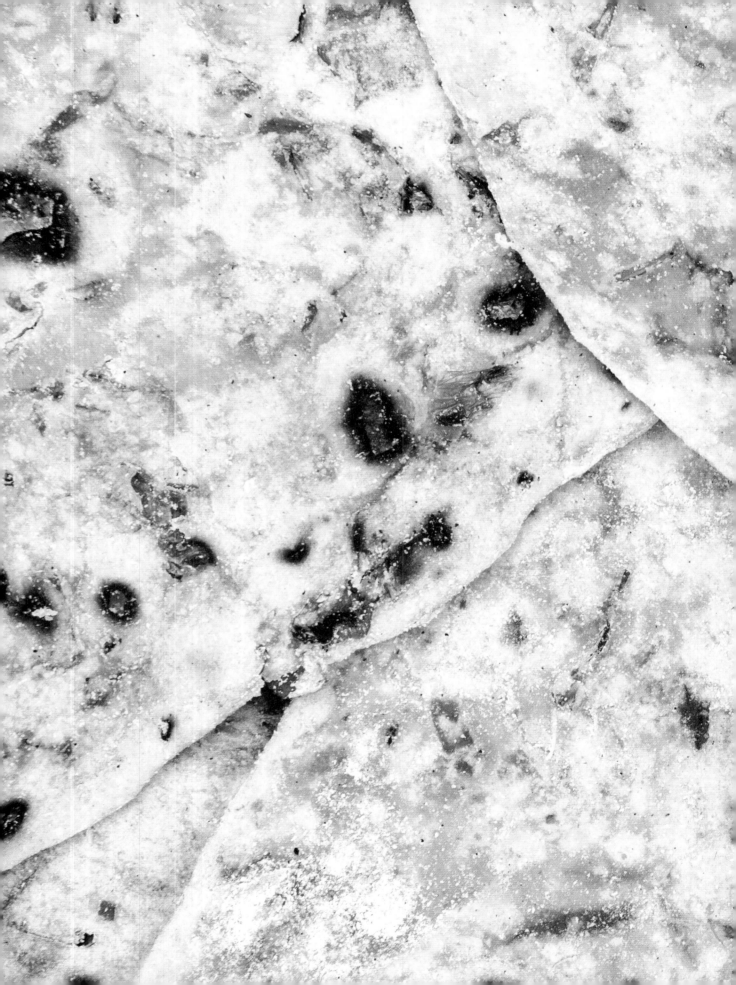

THE
PANTRY

BLACK CARDAMOM / SEA SALT / CINNAMON LEAVES / TOMATO / GARLIC

CHICKPEA

FRAGRANT CHICKPEA SOUP

200 g (7 oz) dried chickpeas (soaked in cold water for 24 hours)

CHARACTER

A seductively perfumed, smoky, deep, and unusual blend.

VARIATIONS

The aromatic blend can also be used with other pulses and grains.

AROMATIC BLEND #33

400 g (14 oz) overripe tomatoes, roughly chopped
3 (15 g) cloves garlic, peeled
5 (5 g) black cardamom pods (see p. 277)
5 (1.5 g) whole dried cinnamon leaves (see p. 278)
4 g (1 tsp) sea salt, plus more for seasoning
600 ml (2½ cups) cold water, for boiling

Freshly ground black pepper
50 g (1 ¾ oz) cold unsalted butter (topping)

After several weeks of experimentation, there is no doubt: The pressure cooker delivers the tastiest, most silky-soft and creamy chickpeas. The benefit of using a pressure cooker is that you save time and also preserve valuable aromas. What's more, the chickpeas, as they are tightly sealed in the pressure cooker, hold more flavor notes than if you used a saucepan with a lid. This soup is very easy to make, and is a great hit during the cold months of the year, when you'll need to replace the fresh tomatoes with high-quality canned tomatoes. It keeps well for up to four days, and just gets better. You can naturally add all kinds of thinly cut vegetables and fresh herbs.

AROMATIC BLEND

Put the tomatoes, garlic, black cardamom pods, cinnamon leaves, sea salt, and water in a pressure cooker. Durability: Use immediately. Makes 1 l (4 cups)

CHICKPEAS

Rinse, wash, and thoroughly drain the soaked chickpeas then add them to the pressure cooker. Put on the lid and turn up the heat. When the pressure cooker makes 'noise' and sputters with steam, turn down the heat slightly, but make sure there is still plenty of steam coming out of the valve. Cook the chickpeas for 15 minutes then turn off the heat and let stand for at least 30 minutes. The waiting time is important to the taste, so be patient. Just before

serving, season with sea salt and freshly ground black pepper, and add the cold butter. Serve in a large bowl, leaving the cinnamon leaves and black cardamom in as decoration.

Alternatively, the chickpeas can be cooked in a covered pot on the stove for 1–1½ hours, or until tender (using the same amount of water). If too much of the stock boils away, gradually add extra water. Allow the chickpeas to stand for at least 30 minutes, and follow the above procedure for serving.

SEASON: All year round
Starter or soup for 4
Makes 1.2 l (5 cups) soup

SHALLOTS/TURMERIC ROOT/GINGER ROOT/ OLIVE OIL/SAGE/CUMIN

EGG

CRISP-FRIED LIGHT AND FLUFFY OMELET

6 medium eggs

CHARACTER

A warming, sharp, moist, crisp, full-bodied, refined, and harmonious blend with subtle orange notes and Indian attitude.

VARIATIONS

The aromatic blend can also be used with roasted fish, shellfish, and thinly sliced vegetables. Or, add it from the start to rice and grain dishes. It can be fried golden and crispy, and tossed with cabbage, or added to cold, creamy, whole milk yogurt for a spicy, yellow dip.

AROMATIC BLEND #34

30 g (1 oz) shallots, peeled
20 g (4 tsp) fresh ginger with peel
10 g (4 tsp) fresh turmeric with peel
10 g (⅓ oz) fresh sage
2 g (1 tsp) whole cumin seeds
45 ml (3 tbsp) cold-pressed olive oil, for frying
Sea salt

This is a very special egg dish that offers refined aromas and a delicately crunchy texture thanks to its aromatic blend. The omelet should be cooked in plenty of cold-pressed olive oil, so that the base and edges get extra crisp. By using both the stove and the oven, you can ensure the omelet will be luscious in the middle and crisp on top like a Spanish tortilla. This dish is made lightning fast, and all in one go, so be sure to preset the broiler to high, and get the eggs prepped before you start frying the aromatic blend. Also note that the pan you use to cook both the aromatic blend and the omelet must be ovenproof. Any kind of sweet and sour pickles or ketchups make a good addition to the omelet when serving.

AROMATIC BLEND

Put the shallots, ginger, turmeric, sage, and cumin seeds in a food processor and blend until very finely chopped, or chop all the ingredients by hand with a sharp knife. In a 25 cm (10 in) cast iron pan or ovenproof frying pan, heat the cold-pressed olive oil over medium-high heat. Fry the aromatic blend, stirring frequently to prevent burning, for 2–3 minutes, or until evenly golden brown. Durability: Use immediately. Makes 100 ml (7 tbsp).

EGGS

Put the eggs in a small bowl, season with sea salt, and whisk lightly with a fork. Remember to preset the broiler to high, and get the eggs prepped before you start frying the aromatic blend. As soon as the aromatic blend is golden brown, quickly pour the beaten eggs into the middle of the pan, so they automatically mix with the aromatic blend, and don't require any stirring. Reduce the heat slightly and cook for 1 minute, or until the omelet is firm on the bottom and sides but isn't burning. Immediately put the pan under the broiler and broil for 30–60 seconds, or until the omelet bubbles up and turns golden. Alternatively, you can use a larger frying pan (to prevent burning) and fry the omelet completely on the stove (no need to flip it).

SEASON: All year round
Starter or side dish for 4

CHIVE FLOWERS/ROSE PETALS/BUTTER/CARAWAY FLOWERS/SEA SALT/WATER

FLOUR

SUMMER FLATBREAD CHAPATIS

250 g (9 oz) plain wheat flour, plus more for sprinkling

CHARACTER

A warm, green, and elegant floral blend that's reminiscent of summer, with delicate herbal and subtle onion notes.

VARIATIONS

The aromatic blend can also be used with others types of flour. Try replacing some of the plain wheat flour with, for example, spelt, rye, oat, or barley flour. Depending on the flour mixture you use, you may need to adjust the amount of water.

AROMATIC BLEND #35

Approx. 130 ml (9 tbsp) tepid water, plus more as needed
50 g (1 ¾ oz) fresh edible flowers
50 g (1 ¾ oz) unsalted butter, melted
2 g (½ tsp) sea salt

Flatbread chapatis are easy to make, and require less than a minute in a hot pan. And with edible flowers folded into the batter, they taste of elegant incense and floral heaven. It is certainly not silly to use flowers directly in food. When quickly exposed to high heat, as with these chapatis, their aromas are released in the best possible way, while being protected by a thin layer of dough. I am using a lot of fresh flowers for this recipe, and they should certainly not be chopped, as the flowers are practically stamped into the dough during the lengthy kneading process. You can use different flowers, depending on the season and where you live, and in winter, the flowers can be replaced by crushed spices. Last but not least, if you use whole wheat flour, you'll need to add additional water to the dough.

AROMATIC BLEND

Put the tepid water, flowers, butter, and sea salt in a large bowl or the bowl of a stand mixer fitted with the dough hook attachment. Durability: Use immediately. Makes 480 ml (2 cups).

FLOUR

Add the flour to the aromatic blend and knead by hand or with the dough hook for 10 minutes, or until pliable, elastic, and smooth. It doesn't matter if the dough is a bit sticky, but you should be able to remove it from your fingers or the dough hook fairly easily. If it's too dry, gradually add more tepid water. Place a damp, clean cloth on top, and let rise in a warm place for 30 minutes (the dough will hardly rise).

Divide the dough into 10–12 clumps of 40 g (8 tbsp) each (depending on what size chapati will fit in your cast iron pan). On a lightly floured surface, use a lightly floured rolling pin to roll each portion into a thin round that's 20 cm (8 in) in diameter. When rolling, sprinkle additional flour as needed. Stack the chapatis, dusting them with a little extra flour to prevent sticking. If not cooking right away, wrap the chapatis in a damp, clean cloth, and store up to 40 minutes.

When ready to serve, heat a large cast iron pan over high heat. Working with 1 chapati at a time, shake off any excess flour then place the chapati in the hot pan without any fat, and cook, flipping once, for 20–30 seconds per side, or until each side has a few lightly burned spots. The chapatis should not be cooked until crisp; they should be soft and elastic. As soon as the chapatis are done, wrap them tightly in a clean cloth to keep warm. Repeat with the remaining chapatis and serve immediately.

SEASON: All year round
Side or snack for 4
Makes 10–12 chapatis

CARDAMOM / TOMATO / TURMERIC / GINGER ROOT / CEYLON CINNAMON / CUMIN / CORIANDER SEED / SHALLOTS / CHILI / GARLIC

LENTIL

QUICK AROMATIC LENTIL SOUP

200 g (7 oz) red or yellow lentils

CHARACTER

A mild, warm, slightly sharp, and very aromatic blend.

VARIATIONS

The aromatic blend can also be used when cooking other legumes, such as beans and pulses, as well as rice and grains. Or, you can use it with baked vegetables.

AROMATIC BLEND #36

3 g (1½ tsp) whole cumin seeds
3 g (1½ tsp) whole coriander seeds
2.5 cm (1 in) (2 g) Ceylon cinnamon stick
6 (1.5 g) cardamom pods
0.3 g (⅛ tsp) chili flakes
500 g (18 oz) coarsely chopped very ripe cherry tomatoes
100 g (3 ½ oz) coarsely chopped shallots
4 (20 g) cloves garlic, coarsely chopped
15 g (1 tbsp) finely chopped ginger with peel
1 g (½ tsp) ground turmeric

800 ml (3⅓ cups) cold water
Sea salt
100 g (3 ½ oz) coarsely chopped creamed coconut (topping)
200 g (7 oz) spinach (topping)
Freshly ground black pepper

Nutritious, filling, aromatic, and inexpensive, this soup is a year-round classic in our house. In the cold months, you can substitute high-quality canned tomatoes for the cherry tomatoes. In early spring, when wild garlic is in season, use it in place of the spinach. Be generous, as garlic really works in this soup. Otherwise, you can use bok choy or regular cabbage. Creamed coconut is a hard, white block consisting of 100 percent mature coconut flesh, which has been ground up, dehydrated, and compressed. It makes the soup creamier and has a softening effect not unlike butter, so it's best added at the very end of cooking. If you happen to have fresh turmeric root, you can finely grate 2 g (½ tsp) and use it in place of the ground turmeric.

AROMATIC BLEND

Put the cumin seeds, coriander seeds, cinnamon, cardamom pods, and chili flakes in an electric coffee grinder or a mortar and pestle and to grind to a fine powder. Put the powder in a medium bowl. Add the cherry tomatoes, shallots, garlic, ginger, and turmeric and toss to combine. Durability: Use the same day. Makes 720 ml (3 cups).

LENTILS

Wash the lentils under cold water then drain. Put the lentils in a large saucepan, add the aromatic blend and the cold water, and season with sea salt. Bring to a boil then reduce the heat to medium-low and simmer, covered, for 30 minutes, or until the lentils are cooked. If the soup gets too thick, gradually add a little water. If desired, purée the soup coarsely or very finely in a blender or food processor then return it to the saucepan. To serve, bring the soup to a boil then add the creamed coconut and spinach and continue boiling for a few minutes, or until the spinach is cooked but still has bite; season with freshly ground black pepper.

SEASON: All year round
Starter for 4–6
Makes 1.7 l (7 cups) soup

STAR ANISE/APPLE CIDER VINEGAR/KUMQUATS/ GINGER ROOT/JALAPEÑO CHILI/WHITE SUGAR/SEA SALT/GARLIC/WATER

RICE

SWEET AND SOUR RICE

200 g (7 oz) basmati rice

CHARACTER

A spicy and slightly sharp blend with subtle bitterness, warming anise notes, and a Chinese feel to it.

VARIATIONS

The aromatic blend can also be used as a kind of wok sauce, added in the last minutes when stir-frying seafood, meat, poultry, or vegetables. Or, you can use it to make a side dish, with grains and pulses, broccoli, cauliflower, and Chinese or other cabbage varieties.

AROMATIC BLEND #37

150 g (5 ¼ oz) ripe kumquats
5 (25 g) cloves garlic, thinly sliced
1 (15 g) fresh jalapeño chili with seeds, thinly sliced
40 g (1 ⅖ oz) ginger, peeled and cut into thin matchsticks
2 (2.5 g) whole star anise
12 g (3 tsp) sea salt
100 g (3 ½ oz) white sugar
100 ml (7 tbsp) unfiltered apple cider vinegar
100 ml (7 tbsp) water

200 g (7 oz) spinach with stems (topping)
Cold-pressed olive oil, for frying

This rice dish is filling, full-bodied, and highly aromatic. If you can get hold of spinach leaves with stems, they provide some extra juicy crunch. Kumquats are small, but they pack a powerful punch. The small, orange-yellow, oval-shaped citrus fruits are sweet, with just the right amount of bitterness. That means you can eat them raw, without any kind of preparation, which is delightful. Taste your kumquats before you buy them, as they can vary enormously in taste. The recipe makes quite a lot of the aromatic blend, but once you start chopping, it's hardly worth it to make less, and it will keep for a week or two in the refrigerator. You can use all kinds of rice for this dish—just adjust the time and quantity according to the variety you choose.

AROMATIC BLEND

Cut the kumquats into quarters and remove the seeds. In a medium saucepan, combine the kumquats with the rest of the aromatic blend ingredients and bring to a boil. Cover and continue boiling, stirring occasionally, for 20 minutes, or until the mixture has a syrupy consistency. Pour the aromatic blend into a clean preserves jar and let cool to room temperature. Durability: 1–2 weeks refrigerated. Makes 300 ml (1 ¼ cups).

RICE

Wash the rice thoroughly in fresh cold water then soak in fresh cold water for 30 minutes. Drain the rice then put it in a medium saucepan with 400 ml (1 ⅔ cups) fresh cold water, cover, and bring to a boil. Remove the lid, reduce the heat, and cook the rice, without stirring, for 10–15 minutes, or until air holes form on the surface. Once the air holes stop giving off water or bubbles, take the rice off the heat, cover, and let stand for 10 minutes. When ready to serve, sauté the spinach in a very hot pan with a little cold-pressed olive oil for 2–3 minutes, or until wilted. Top the steaming rice with the spinach and the aromatic blend (room temperature).

SEASON: January–May
Starter or side dish for 4

CEYLON CINNAMON / CHOCOLATE / APRICOT KERNELS / WALNUTS / PISTACHIOS / CLOVES / AQUAVIT / ALLSPICE

DRIED FRUIT

FRUIT SALAMI DE LUXE

1 kg (2 ¼ lb) mixed dried fruit, such as dates and figs

CHARACTER

A warm, elegant, highly aromatic, full-bodied, and fresh blend, with a crunchy texture, outstanding aroma, and winter mood.

VARIATIONS

The aromatic blend can also be used with other dried fruit and nuts.

AROMATIC BLEND #38

150 g (5 ¼ oz) dark chocolate (min. 80%)
100 g (3 ½ oz) walnuts
100 g (3 ½ oz) pistachios
100 g (3 ½ oz) apricot kernels or almonds
4 cm (1 ½ in) (3 g) stick Ceylon cinnamon
15 (3 g) whole allspice berries
15 (2 g) whole cloves
100 ml (7 tbsp) aquavit or vodka

An outstanding confectionery, with no added sugar, this is, without a doubt, my favorite Christmas candy. My preferred combination is 750 g (26 oz) figs and 250 g (8¾ oz) Medjool dates. Use dried fruit that is still fairly soft. Don't bother halving the portion—it's not worth it, as the salami will keep for several months. The dried fruit can be chopped by hand, but it's hard work. Use a food processor instead, and be patient, because even that will have to work pretty hard. Serve the salami in thin slices with tea, toddy, coffee, or hot chocolate. Be sure to plan ahead, as the salami need to dry out for 1 to 1 ½ months.

AROMATIC BLEND

Coarsely chop the chocolate, walnuts, pistachios, and apricot kernels and combine in a large bowl. Put the cinnamon, allspice berries, and cloves in an electric coffee grinder and grind to a fine powder. Add the powder to the chocolate and nut mixture and toss to combine. Durability: Use the same day. Makes 750 ml (3 ¼ cups).

DRIED FRUITS

If using figs, cut off the hard stems. If using dates, remove the hard tops and discard any seeds. Cut the dried fruit into thin slices. This is important; otherwise, the food processor cannot blend the fruit evenly. Put the fruit in a large bowl, add the aquavit, stir, and let stand for at least 1 hour but no more than 2 hours. Working in 3–4 batches, blend the fruit in a food processor.

Be patient. The mixture is heavy and tough, but it must be thoroughly blended or you won't be able to roll it into salamis. Put the blended fruit in a large bowl, add the aromatic blend, and press the mass together with your hands.

Divide the mixture into 3 even portions then form each portion into a salami about 5 cm (2 in) in diameter. Wrap tightly in 2 layers of parchment paper, so the salami can breathe and any moisture will evaporate as the salami dry. Leave in a cool, dry place for at least 1–1½ months, or until the salami is firm enough to cleanly cut into slices. Keep wrapped and store in a cool, dry place. The finished salami will keep for several months.

SEASON: All year round
Makes 3 (25 cm / 10 in) logs or 150 slices

CANE SUGAR / LAVENDER FLOWERS / CARDAMOM / HIBISCUS FLOWERS

YOGURT

FLOWER YOGURT

1 l (4 cups) plain whole milk yogurt

CHARACTER

A refreshing, cooling, and addictive blend, with elegant floral notes that call forth memories of late summer berries.

VARIATIONS

The aromatic blend can also be used in whipped cream and mousses, as a cake topping, and on top of your morning muesli. You can also fold it into ice cream bases, use it to add flavor to pear and apple pies, or sprinkle it on ripe fresh fruit.

AROMATIC BLEND #39

45 g (3 tbsp) light cane sugar
15 g (½ oz) dried whole hibiscus flowers (see p. 223)
0.8 g (1 tsp) dried lavender flowers (see p. 223)
12 (3 g) cardamom pods

Avoid acidic, low-fat dairy products, and instead choose a whole milk yogurt that is sweet, mild, and creamy. If the yogurt isn't mixed too thoroughly, you will experience pockets of intense floral flavor buried between the yogurt layers. A mortar and pestle won't produce the super-fine texture that's essential to this aromatic blend, so use an electric coffee grinder.

AROMATIC BLEND

Put the light cane sugar, hibiscus flowers, lavender flowers, and cardamom pods in an electric coffee grinder and grind to a very fine powder that has the consistency of icing sugar. Durability: 2–3 weeks at room temperature. Makes 60 g (2 oz).

YOGURT

To serve, use 15 g (3 tbsp) of the aromatic blend for every 250 ml (1 cup) yogurt. Pour the yogurt into small bowls, add the aromatic blend, making sure not to mix it too thoroughly, and serve.

SEASON: All year round
Snack or dessert for 4

CANE SUGAR / BAKING POWDER / BUTTER / SPELT FLOUR / GOLDEN SYRUP / CARAWAY

FEATHERLIGHT SEED COOKIES

150 g (5 ¼ oz) mixed seeds, such as ⅓ black sesame seeds, ⅓ chia seeds, ⅓ yellow linseed

CHARACTER

A sweet, mellow, and delicate blend; it has an understated hay aroma, elegant nutty notes, and a pleasantly crunchy texture.

VARIATIONS

The aromatic blend can also be used with other dried seeds, as well as dried fruit, nuts, and flaked cereals.

AROMATIC BLEND #40

3 g (1 tsp) whole caraway seeds
130 g (4 ½ oz) unsalted butter
40 g (2 tbsp) golden syrup or black treacle
130 g (4 ½ oz) sifted spelt flour
100 g (3 ½ oz) light cane sugar
2.5 g (1 tsp) baking powder

Very tasty, ultra-crisp, and easy-to-make, these cookies are an elegant match for cheese, not least because of their warm caraway flavor. But, they are even better stuck into vanilla, banana, or chocolate ice cream, or with a cup of hot chocolate, coffee, or Assam tea. They might seem too soft when first out of the oven, but as the cookies cool, they become hard and brittle, so be careful not to over-bake them. It's a good idea to make a test batch, with one tray of cookies, before you finish baking the rest. You can buy sifted spelt flour. It has a fine texture that's similar to plain wheat flour, and not as coarse as whole spelt flour.

AROMATIC BLEND

Heat a small frying pan over high heat. Add the caraway seeds and dry-roast for 5–15 seconds, or until fragrant and beginning to take on color. Immediately put the caraway seeds in a mortar and pestle and grind to a medium-fine powder. Put the powder, along with the butter and golden syrup, in a small saucepan and warm over low heat until the butter is melted. In a large bowl, whisk together the sifted spelt flour, light cane sugar, and baking powder. Add the hot butter mixture and stir until combined. Durability: Use immediately, while still hot. Makes 350 ml (1½ cups).

SEEDS

Add the seeds to the hot aromatic blend and stir until combined. The consistency will be loose and greasy, and will look as though it is about to fall apart. Don't worry—this is normal. Let the dough stand for 10 minutes. Use a measuring spoon to divide the dough into clumps of about 20 g (15 ml) each. Arrange the clumps on 2–4 parchment paper–lined baking sheets and use the palm of your hand to press them into smooth, completely flat circles about 9–10 cm (3½–4 in) in diameter. Make sure there is a little space between the cookies (approx. 2 cm/¾ in). Bake in a preheated 165°C (325°F) oven for 10–12 minutes, or until the cookies start to develop an even, dark golden color. Let cool completely then store in a tightly sealed container in a cool, dark place for 7–8 days.

SEASON: All year round
Makes 22–24 cookies

EDIBLE FLOWERS— PRECIOUS MOMENTS

Suddenly you are struck by a fragrance and the world stands still. Whatever you had in your head a moment before has vanished. You haven't been talking to anyone. You are just moving and breathing like you always do. You're out in the garden, where the aromatic substances from pollen and plants fill your lungs every time you take a breath. These are fleeting moments and filled with the finest aromatic compounds. The fragrance of fully blooming flowers disappears after just a few hours, unless it's pinned down in a substance. And the most precious flowers do not give up their innermost secrets easily. This makes working in the kitchen a fascinating business.

Flowers are not just fragrance and flavor. When flowers are added to food, an aromatic tour de force begins. One minute you might have a headache and in the next you feel giddy and happy. Not even herbal leaves can compete. These are stimuli working at a staggeringly high sensory level, and consisting of complex aromatic compounds that bounce around inside your nose and mouth, making you remember moments, feelings, and sensations from the past. They give you pause for thought! At the same time, all these aromas help cleanse your mouth after every sip and bite you take. And when you finish eating, you're left with a healing sensation in body and mind.

All the flowers of edible plants can be used in food, whether they come from herbs, fruit bushes and trees, or vegetables. Cabbages and lettuce that are allowed to go to seed also produce flowers and they taste wonderful. Some flowers can do a little of everything, while others require more instinctive consideration. Flowers that seem extremely delicate and graceful in their fragrance can easily end up dominating a dish. In some recipes, flowers can be added from the start and make all the difference—sweet and sour sautéed bok choy (p. 36) is a perfect example. Other times, flowers can be used for a subtle effect on top of a dish, where they are hardly prepared at all, such as in the roasted zucchini salad (p. 168). Fresh flowers can also be enjoyed without great fuss, simply by drawing the nectar out of them as though you were a bee, drinking the water that lies in the roses after a downpour, or by steeping them in hot water to make a tea.

HONEY—FLOWER NECTAR AND POLLEN

Plants, trees, and bushes cannot move around like animals and human beings. With the help of the wind and insects, especially bees, their genes can meet up in a second flower, even if they're far apart. Honey is a natural product that bees make from the nectar and pollen they collect from the flowers they pollinate. Honey is therefore unique in that floral fragrances from near and far are brought together in a nectar that retains most of the original aromas, thanks to the hardworking bees.

Honey can be a dominant and difficult ingredient to work with, but it is an interesting one, as the influence of just a single flower is often enough to create disorder or balance when added to food. Imagine a field of blue lavender, or an old orange grove filled with creamy white flowers. And when the wild flowers are in bloom, it's even better, because of the complexity of the aromatic substances. Where I live, near the edge of the woods, there is hawthorn, blackthorn, elder, blackberries, and fir. And by the sea, I can find rosehip, heather, thyme, and an arsenal of rare plants in bloom. This makes for a rich assortment of honeys that can be used in a variety of different ways.

WHEN FLOWERS ARE ADDED TO FOOD, AN AROMATIC TOUR DE FORCE BEGINS

Masculine and distinctive honeys are perfect for like-minded ingredients, such as chili, ginger, turmeric, and garlic, while feminine and delicate honeys are obviously good for desserts and salads. Good honey is raw (unheated) and unfiltered. Used intelligently, it can turn a dish upside down and add something exotic that you won't get from other ingredients.

POLLEN

If you have a garden, you can pick the flowers and use their pollen in your cooking. The best pollen comes from the first flowering. Pick the flowers on sunny days, as soon as the dew has gone, but always check first to make sure all the insects are gone! The aromas in the pollen are extremely porous, so they should be added at the very end, when the flowers are shaken over a finished dish. No matter what plant it comes from, pollen provides a warm and subtle effect that mainly suits milder vegetable, potato, rice, and pasta dishes that won't overwhelm the aromatic substances. The yellow flowers of bronze fennel (*Foeniculum vulgare v. Rubrum*) always delight, and are fairly easy to obtain. If you prefer, put a piece of parchment paper on the table and shake the flowers over it then add the pollen to your dish. It can be used as a topping on mild yogurt, hot oatmeal, or fruit compote, and on ice cream or cold mousses and cold puddings. Or, try mixing pollen into a glaze for cakes and cookies. If you don't have enough pollen or just want an easier approach, simply chop whole flowers very finely with a sharp knife, and use them right away and in the same manner.

A SPLASH OF FLOWER WATER

Flower water is a very quick and relatively inexpensive way to give your dishes a floral atmosphere. It's a colorless liquid, contains minimal sweetness, and has several advantages. The finest flower water is made from fresh flowers, with rose and orange blossom water being the most popular for cooking. They're like a mixture of a simple perfume and a fine boiled candy drop. The notes are intense, warm, feminine, and a little giddy.

You can make your own flower water from fresh roses, but it's a waste of time and resources, as it will never contain the porous and delicate top notes that the distillation process draws from the flowers. True flower water is, in fact, a by-product of the production of one hundred percent natural essential oils that are extracted from flowers using a gentle steam bath. It's a highly efficient process, and retains as much as possible of the plant's integrity. The steam collects condensed water and oil droplets in a boiler, and those are then passed through a filter that separates the water (flower hydrolate / distillate) from the essential oil. The exclusive rose oil is now called rose otto or attar of roses, and is one of the most coveted and expensive essential oils. One drop is equal to sixty fresh roses. This is

why there are no inexpensive rose oils on the market—either you buy the real thing, or you buy something else that resembles it. The same applies to the flower water. Take a close look at the label; there should only be two ingredients, water and rose flower hydrolate (distillate). Inexpensive versions are made by mixing water with alcohol and a little rose oil. There is a huge difference in quality between expensive and inexpensive flower water, which may explain why flower water isn't commonly used. The worst kinds tend to smell and taste like shoddy cheap perfume, while genuine flower water is elegant, and can be used not just in Middle Eastern cooking, but in all sorts of dishes from about the world.

Genuine or not, flower water tends to vary greatly in concentration. Put a few drops in a glass of water and assess it before cooking with it. Flower water is both intense and volatile. To maintain its full glory, it should be combined with fat or sugar, or preferably both. You can use flower water in glazes for cakes and cookies. Or put it in ice cream, sorbet, juices, and drinks. If a cake is a little dry, try brushing it with a mixture of boiled citrus juice, sugar, and flower water. Or, sprinkle flower water over fruit, salads, and vegetable dishes. You can also add flower water to sweet-and-sour fruit chutneys and jams for your morning toast. How much flower water to use is a matter of taste, and depends entirely on the strength, but the rule of thumb is 1 to 2 tsp (5 to 10 ml) per portion or person.

FRESH ROSES VS. DRIED ROSES

There are hundreds of rose varieties, but when it comes to making the precious rose oil used by the perfume industry, there are only a few varieties of importance. One is the Damask rose (*Rosa damascena*), which is mainly grown in Bulgaria, Turkey, and Iran, while the other is the Provence rose, also known as Rose de Mai (*Rosa centifolia*), which is cultivated in France, Morocco, and Egypt. Another rose that is beautiful and quite free of charge is wild rose hip (*Rosa rugosa*). It's magenta-colored, highly fragrant, and found along the coasts of Scandinavia, Siberia, Korea, and Japan.

Whatever their name or origin, all fragrant roses can be used in cooking, as long as they have not been sprayed with pesticides. Fresh rose petals are both gentle and robust. The petals have enough power to withstand being grilled or exposed to short periods of intense heat. You will miss out on all the porous and delicate top notes, but it makes no difference, as they are almost impossible to pin down anyway. If you add the petals at the end—in a very hot salad that has been baked or fried—the aromatic compounds will come alive from the temperature, and spring straight into the salad at once, without going to waste. Dried rose buds are different, and do different things. They possess much more warmth and sweetness. They have a refined floral fragrance and taste, although it can sometimes be a little old-fashioned. Dried rose buds have a far stronger taste than fresh rose buds, which is why they're suitable for dishes that require longer cooking times. They can easily be ground into a powder, and combined with other ingredients to use with meat, poultry, pork, lamb, fish, vegetables, and sweet dishes. Get dried rosebuds rather than rose petals, as the latter lose their aroma too quickly. If you wish to use rose petals in a dish, remove the stems and divide the leaves carefully. And if you are going to grind rose buds into a powder, leave the stalks on.

FRESH LAVENDER FLOWERS VS. DRIED LAVENDER FLOWERS

Genuine fresh blue lavender (*Lavandula angustifolia*) is like a grand French perfume. This is mainly due to the large amounts of cooling balsamic notes of camphor, menthol, citrus, and eucalyptus, all aromas that are lovely in pastries, cakes, juices, cocktails, mousses, sweet rice dishes, and ice cream, as well as with fruit. When fresh flowers are dried, the aromatic substances are weakened—there's no getting around that. However, as lavender flowers are so voluminous, they will still have plenty of character, even if the aroma experience is considerably milder, sweeter, and slightly dusty. In winter, they add a little floral joy to both savory and sweet dishes, and can be used with meat, fish, vegetables, fruit, and pastries. The taste of lavender goes well with fresh rosemary, cardamom pods, dried rose buds, and fresh spearmint, either in combination or added separately. On a bad day, regardless of whether the flower is fresh or dried, it can produce an unfortunate soapy taste, but that only happens if you are overconfident and use too much.

DRIED HIBISCUS FLOWERS

Hibiscus (*Hibiscus sabdariffa l. 'roselle'*) is a high-class floral drama. The dried, ruby-red flowers possess warmth and a sharp fruit aroma, while their taste is refreshing, with an elegant, bitter aftertaste that's never too much or too little. After a few seconds, you experience a whirlwind of citrus notes that call to mind ripe late-summer berries, and usually make it unnecessary to add any additional acidity. Hibiscus is also easy to work with, relatively inexpensive, and adds a charming red hue to dishes. The flower is fantastic when added to fruit juice and

SUDDENLY YOU ARE STRUCK BY A FRAGRANCE AND THE WORLD STANDS STILL. WHATEVER YOU HAD IN YOUR HEAD A MOMENT BEFORE HAS VANISHED

sorbets. The only flaw I can find is that hibiscus isn't suitable for dishes that have to keep for more than six months, that is, canned and pickled foods, as it slowly changes course, becoming tired and flat in taste. If the dried flowers are ground as fine as powdered sugar, hibiscus can be used as a sharp and refined topping to be sprinkled on poultry, pork, lamb, fish, seafood, vegetables, or fruit. The powder can also be used in desserts, and is especially suitable for those that are overpoweringly sweet, like meringues. If hibiscus is boiled in water, or exposed to heat, even more aromatic substances are released. The liquid turns a beautiful dark magenta color that will intoxicate anyone. I use hibiscus flowers in relatively large quantities, and recommend you do too; otherwise, you'll never experience their full drama.

RIPE
FRUITS

CLOVE / POTATO STARCH /
CANE SUGAR / CEYLON
CINNAMON / CORIANDER
SEED / GINGER / ALLSPICE

APPLE

DEEP-FRIED AROMATIC APPLE FRITTERS

4 apples (700 g / 25 oz)

CHARACTER

A blend with Christmas spirit and winter atmosphere; piquant and deep with dominant warming spices.

VARIATIONS

The aromatic blend can also be used with pears, beets, potatoes, or carrots, and in fruit pies, cakes, and cookies (without the potato starch).

AROMATIC BLEND #41

5 g (1 tsp) light cane sugar
2.5 cm (1 in) (2 g) stick Ceylon cinnamon
2 g (1 tsp) whole coriander seeds
6 (1 g) whole allspice berries
5 (0.5 g) whole cloves
2 g (1 tsp) ground ginger
20 g (2 tbsp) potato starch, plus 50 g (5 tbsp), for coating

1.5 l (6 cups) cold-pressed neutral oil, such as canola or peanut, for frying
Powdered sugar (topping)
Maple syrup (topping)

These fritters taste and smell of Christmas, and evoke memories of freshly baked apple pie and hot mulled cider. They're also highly aromatic and make for a relatively fast dessert. I have held back on the sugar, so that the finished apple fritters can be given a good shot of powdered sugar and maple syrup at the very end.

AROMATIC BLEND

Put the light cane sugar, Ceylon cinnamon, coriander seeds, allspice berries, and cloves in an electric coffee grinder and grind to a fine powder. Put the powder in a small bowl, add the ginger and potato starch (20 g / 2 tbsp), and stir to combine. Durability: Use immediately. Makes 50 ml (3 ¼ tbsp).

APPLES

Coarsely grate the apples with a grater, and discard the cores and seeds. Carefully press all the juice out of the grated apples using your hands. Do this several times until no more juice flows out, and remember to enjoy the freshly pressed apple juice. Put the pressed apples into a medium bowl. Add the aromatic blend and use your hands to mix it with the apples; let stand for 10 minutes.

Use your hands to press and roll the mixture into 13–16 balls (approx. 25 g / 1 ½ tbsp per

ball). Sprinkle the remaining potato starch (50 g / 5 tbsp) onto a piece of parchment paper, roll the balls in the starch until completely coated, and set aside.

Heat the cold-pressed neutral oil in a wok to 180°C (360°F). In two batches, fry the fritters for 6–10 minutes, or until dark golden and crisp. Place the fritters on a rack and serve piping hot with generous amounts of powdered sugar and maple syrup.

If the frying oil is kept under 200°C (395°F) it can be reused several times. Cool the oil slightly then pour it through a coffee filter or fine-mesh sieve. Keep the oil in a clean jar, cool and dry, until the next time you need it.

SEASON: August–March
Dessert or snack for 4
Makes 13–16 fritters

ORANGE BLOSSOM WATER /
ANISE SEED / VANILLA /
SAFFRON / WATER / CANE
SUGAR / LEMON JUICE /
BITTER ALMOND

PEACH

PERFUMED PEACH SORBET

8 very ripe peaches (900 g / 2 lb)

CHARACTER

A Middle East-inspired blend that's elegant, feminine, warm, and fragrant; it offers an intense sensory experience that will definitely put you in a good mood.

VARIATIONS

The aromatic blend can also be used to make sorbet with pears, apples, apricots, plums, and figs. Alternatively, it can be used for poaching or baking fruit. Without fruit, the aromatic blend can be reduced to a syrup and poured over any pastries that need a little tangy sweetness or a bit of moisture.

AROMATIC BLEND #42

1.2 g (¼ tsp) whole anise seeds
300 g (10 ½ oz) light cane sugar
¼ genuine vanilla pod, seeds scraped
1 (1 g) finely grated bitter almond (optional) (see p. 277)
0.1 g (⅛ tsp) saffron threads
200 ml (13 tbsp) freshly squeezed lemon juice
100 ml (7 tbsp) water
60 ml (4 tbsp) orange blossom water (see p. 222)

This sorbet has a highly aromatic flavor that immediately calls to mind the dessert repertoire of the Middle East. Good-quality orange blossom water (neroli oil extracted from bitter oranges and mixed with water) is a must, if the sorbet is to hit the spot. Allow the sorbet mixture to stand overnight, and the almond aroma will increase significantly. The sorbet has a wonderful profusion of taste, so a couple of scoops per person is plenty. The sorbet mixture, unfrozen, resembles a lovely thick compote. Serve it with cakes, enjoy it with some drained yogurt, or use it as a layer in cakes.

AROMATIC BLEND

Heat a small frying pan over high heat. Add the anise seeds and dry-roast for 5–15 seconds, or until fragrant and beginning to take on color. Immediately put the anise seeds in a mortar and pestle and grind to a fine powder. Put the powder in a large saucepan, along with the light cane sugar, vanilla seeds and pod, bitter almond, if using, and saffron. Add the lemon juice, water, and orange blossom water, and stir to combine. Durability: Use the same day. Makes 600 ml (2½ cups).

PEACHES

Cut the peaches in half, remove the stones, and cut into chunks (the cleaned weight should be approx. 800 g / 1 ¾ lb). Add the peaches to the saucepan with the aromatic blend, cover, and bring to a boil. Reduce the heat and simmer, covered, for 5–10 minutes, or until the peaches are soft. Cool the mixture then refrigerate until cold and process in an ice cream machine. Serve a couple of scoops per person in small fine glasses.

Using an ice cream machine produces the best results, but this sorbet can easily be made without one. Pour the cold sorbet mixture into a wide, low mold and freeze, stirring occasionally, for about 8 hours. Before serving, remove the sorbet from the freezer and stir until it has a soft texture.

SEASON: June–September
Dessert for 4–6
Makes 1 l (4 cups) sorbet

HIBISCUS FLOWERS / CHILI / SEA SALT FLAKES

MELON

MELON SALAD

1 kg (2 ¼ lb) ripe melon

CHARACTER
A sharp, spicy, and fresh blend, with floral notes and the flavor of summer berries.

VARIATIONS
The aromatic blend can also be used with ripe mango, pear, apple, apricot, or cucumber.

AROMATIC BLEND #43
30 g (1 oz) dried whole hibiscus flowers (see p. 223)
2 g (1 tsp) chili flakes
2 g (½ tsp) sea salt flakes

Food really can be this simple and taste this good! This is a thirst-quenching and startlingly fresh fruit salad that is inspired by Mexico, where mango sprinkled with chili, lime, and salt is served on the street, and enjoyed as a snack throughout the day. My aromatic blend serves the same purpose, but it gets a little help from hibiscus flowers, and doesn't use lime. The flowers provide warmth and sharpness, and lend notes of late summer berries. You can use cantaloupe, Charentais, or Galia melons, but it's very important that the fruit be ripe and full of sweetness; otherwise, the combination won't work.

AROMATIC BLEND
Put the hibiscus flowers, chili flakes, and sea salt flakes in an electric coffee grinder and grind to a fine powder. Durability: 1–2 weeks at room temperature. Makes: 30 g (1 oz).

MELON
Halve the melons and scrape out the seeds. Cut the melon into large wedges, remove the skin, and cut the flesh into chunks. Sprinkle half (15 g / ½ oz) the aromatic blend over the melon, turning the chunks as you sprinkle, then let stand for 10 minutes. Taste the melon and add more aromatic blend, if needed, before serving. Reserve the remaining aromatic blend for another use.

SEASON: July–September
Snack or side dish for 4

APPLE CIDER VINEGAR /
WATER / SEA SALT / LEMON
JUICE / CANOLA OIL / RED
ONION / JUNIPER / BLACK
PEPPERCORN / ALLSPICE /
CANE SUGAR

PEAR

HOT GRILLED PEAR SALAD

4 ripe pears (700 g / 25 oz)

CHARACTER

An old-fashioned blend with elegant sweet and sour flavor; juicy, crunchy, mild, fresh, and aromatic.

VARIATIONS

The aromatic blend can also be used with pickles to make a sweet and sour potato salad, or tossed with finely chopped cabbage to make coleslaw.

AROMATIC BLEND #44

75 ml (⅓ cup) unfiltered apple cider vinegar
50 ml (3 ¼ tbsp) water
45 ml (3 tbsp) freshly squeezed lemon juice
45 g (3 tbsp) light cane sugar
2 g (½ tsp) sea salt
5 (1 g) whole allspice berries
5 (0.5 g) whole juniper berries
5 (0.4 g) whole black peppercorns
130 g (4 ½ oz) red onion, cut into ½-cm (⅛-in) thick rings
30 ml (2 tbsp) cold-pressed neutral oil, such as canola or peanut

Cold-pressed olive oil, for grilling
150 g (5 ¼ oz) halved red grapes (topping)
50 g (1 ¾ oz) lamb's ear salad (topping)
5 g (⅛ oz) fresh oregano (topping)

This is a quick and highly aromatic everyday salad, but for it to be successful, the pears must be ripe and bursting with fruity sweetness. They also need to fully caramelize on the grill, so that the smoky notes really come into their own. If you don't have a grill or grill pan, you can roast the pears in a preheated 220°C (420°F) oven for 10 to 15 minutes, or until caramelized. The fresh oregano may be replaced by basil, spearmint, tarragon, or fennel fronds, and broiled peaches, figs, or melons can substitute for the pears.

AROMATIC BLEND

Put the apple cider vinegar, water, lemon juice, light cane sugar, and sea salt in a small saucepan. Put the allspice berries, juniper berries, and peppercorns on the kitchen table and use something heavy, such as a pestle, to give them a quick, light blow without crushing them. Add to the saucepan and bring to a boil over high heat. Continue boiling until reduced to 75 ml (⅓ cup)—this should take less than 5 minutes—then turn off the heat. Add the red onion to the saucepan, along with the cold-pressed neutral oil. Let stand, covered, at room temperature, for at least 1 hour and preferably overnight. Durability: 1–2 weeks refrigerated. Makes 240 ml (1 cup).

PEARS

Heat a grill pan or grill until burning hot. Cut the pears lengthwise in half, leaving the stem and core intact, then brush with a little cold-pressed olive oil. Grill the pears, cut side down and turning once, for 10–15 minutes, or until tender and beginning to release a little moisture—the pears should not be falling apart. In a large bowl, combine the hot pears with the grapes, lamb's ear salad, and oregano then add the aromatic blend (room temperature), toss to combine, and serve.

SEASON: August–February
Starter or side dish for 4

JUNIPER / ORANGE / APPLE JUICE / ROSEMARY / CEYLON CINNAMON / CLOVES

QUINCE

QUINCE TODDY

2 quinces (500 g / 18 oz)

CHARACTER

A piquant and mouthwatering blend that's full of sweetness, and has subtle resin notes.

VARIATIONS

The cooked toddy can also be whisked with cold-pressed olive oil to make a salad dressing. Or, the aromatic blend (without the quince) can be boiled to a syrupy consistency and used as a sour apple drizzle on pancakes, yogurt, muesli, and baked root vegetables.

AROMATIC BLEND #45

1.5 l (6 cups) unfiltered apple juice
10 g (1½ tbsp) coarsely grated orange zest
6 g (3 tbsp) fresh rosemary needles
2.5 cm (1 in) (2 g) Ceylon cinnamon stick
5 (0.7 g) whole cloves
6 (0.5 g) whole juniper berries

Honey (optional)

Quince is my favorite fruit, because it's exotic, bright yellow, and has a unique, highly fragrant, floral scent and a ripe warm taste. The texture is a whole story in itself, but it can only be experienced if the fruit is boiled or baked for at least three-quarters of an hour. You will be rewarded for your patience with deep notes of fresh fruit and an enchantingly delightful velvety texture. The toddy keeps well for up to a week in the fridge, and may also be mixed with water (use a 1:2 ratio), and enjoyed as refreshing iced tea, with or without honey.

AROMATIC BLEND

Put the apple juice, orange zest, and rosemary needles in a large saucepan. Put the cinnamon, cloves, and juniper berries in a mortar and pestle and grind to a medium-fine powder. Add the powder to the saucepan. Durability: Use the same day. Makes 1.5 l (6 cups).

QUINCE

Wash the quinces and rub away any down from the skin. Coarsely grate the quinces with a grater. Add all the grated quince, including the cores and seeds, because they contain large amounts of pectin/starch, to the saucepan with the aromatic blend. The flesh of the quince will turn dark brown when exposed to oxygen, but this won't affect the appearance or taste if cooked immediately. Bring the mixture to a boil then reduce the heat and simmer gently, covered, for 1 hour. Turn off the heat and let stand for 10 minutes. Pour the toddy through a fine-mesh sieve, pressing hard on the solids. It's important that most of the quince pulp gets pressed through the sieve, as this is what gives the toddy its rich texture, but you can discard the core, seeds, and skin. Serve the toddy hot, possibly sweetened with honey.

SEASON: October–January
Toddy for 6
Makes 1.5 l (6 cups)

ROSE PETALS/CANE SUGAR/WATER/ROSE WATER/CARDAMOM

RHUBARB

CHILLED RHUBARB SOUP

400 g (14 oz) trimmed rhubarb without green tops

CHARACTER

A feminine, delicate, and fragrant blend, with quiet notes of warm rose and plenty of camphor, citrus, and eucalyptus.

VARIATIONS

The aromatic blend can also be used with mango, plums, cherry plums, peaches, and apricots. The fruit soup, made with any fruit, can be used, without the coconut milk, to top yogurt, muesli, ice cream, or pancakes.

AROMATIC BLEND #46

16 (4 g) cardamom pods
175 g (6 ¼ oz) light cane sugar
1 g (1 tbsp) dried rose petals (see p. 222)
100 ml (7 tbsp) water
30 ml (2 tbsp) rose water (see p. 222)

400 ml (1 ⅔ cups) coconut milk (min. 80 % coconut; topping)

Rhubarb has a pure, unique flavor that is deep, sharp, and floral. Go for thin stalks, and look for a variety with low amounts of oxalic acid, so the fruit isn't too tart. As rich coconut milk is absolutely essential for this dish, invest in an extra creamy, good-quality version that contains only two ingredients—coconut and water—with a minimum of 80 percent coconut. The silky-soft texture and exotic flavor of the coconut milk is tailor-made for tangy rhubarb, and also has the ability to soothe the oxalic acid in the stems. A few hours after boiling, or the next day, the taste will be even better and the soup can be served cold. This is definitely recommended. In June and July, I pick wild roses along the coast, and it is, of course, always worth replacing the dried flowers with fresh rose petals—use 10 g (⅓ oz).

AROMATIC BLEND

Put the cardamom seeds (open the pods and pick out the seeds) in an electric coffee grinder or mortar and pestle and grind to a medium-fine powder. Put the powder, along with the light cane sugar, rose petals, water, and rose water, in a small bowl and set aside. Durability: Use the same day. Makes 180 ml (¾ cup).

RHUBARB

Cut the rhubarb into chunks and put in a medium saucepan. Add the aromatic blend and bring to a boil. Reduce the heat and simmer for 3 minutes, or until the rhubarb is almost tender. Turn off the heat, cover, and let stand for at least 15 minutes, if serving right away, but preferably overnight to allow the spices to release more flavor. When ready to serve, shake the coconut milk, so it's fluffier. Serve the rhubarb hot or cold and topped with plenty of coconut milk.

SEASON: May–July
Dessert for 4

HOMEGROWN LUXURY

Make no mistake: It is really hard work growing your own fruits and vegetables. On the other hand, it's also tremendously rewarding, because you can tailor a selection to your own taste and fragrance preferences. And ingredients that are harvested at the last minute, just before they go into the kitchen, contain the largest and most interesting concentration of aromatic substances. Unpredictability is complexity in action. The choice of variety, climate, soil fertility, cultivation method, harvesting time, and storage all place their stamp on the flavor and nutrient content of the ingredients. Growing your own fruits and vegetables should be both fun and joyful, but you can quickly make simple things very complicated. Knowledge is a great help, although sometimes it hinders us from just using our intuition. Nature is sophisticated. Just being in green surroundings, especially when gardening, will provide answers and knowledge that are communicated through your instincts. For me, this exercise is far more valuable than reading everything in a book. Plus, you also learn to appreciate those enthusiasts who have made it their livelihood to grow healthy and tasty fruits and vegetables for us. If you're successful, it is pure luxury, a gift you can't otherwise get for love or money, as you're an essential part of the creation. These moments are full of care, joy, despair, creativity, scent, and taste that will influence and leave their mark on you in a multitude of ways.

MY LIFE AS A BEE

More than one-third of the plants we eat require insect pollination in order to produce fruit and seeds. In my garden, it's less dramatic. I'll survive whatever happens, but I'll also do everything I can to get even more bees and butterflies into my garden. I'll even steal burrowing bees from the forest—if spring has been too cold for them to wake up—and bring them back to my warm greenhouse. Or, I'll sow and plant specific flowering plants, trees, and shrubs and cultivate my garden organically. These are all decisions that help attract more insects, and over the years, it's helped create a lot of life in my garden. Keep in mind that chemical fertilizers and pesticides have an adverse effect on an ingredient's aroma and taste. They counteract

nature's aesthetics, and have a negative impact on you, me, and the bees.

Pollination starts in April, inside the greenhouse, where there is an apricot tree and a peach tree. I go around with a little brush made of boar hair, and play bee. But it hasn't always been like that. For the first few years, I only got a few pieces of fruit, or none at all. I didn't realize that you need bees and pollination, as the trees really ought to be self-pollinating. If you grow fruit trees under glass, in a cooler region, as I do, most of the bees will be asleep at pollination time, because there is still a risk of frost. Thus, hand pollination makes for a much better harvest. Pollination time lasts three to four weeks, when every day, new, delicate, creamy white and pink flowers open up to be pollinated. In the beginning, I found it rather stressful, because you have to be extremely careful with the brush, as you jump from flower to flower, or else the stem breaks and the flower falls off. Today, it is more of a meditative process, because I know what to expect if I do my best. And I also really do get help from the bees, as soon as the temperature rises and the door to the garden can be left ajar. July brings juice-laden, sun-ripened fruits of the perfect temperature. It's pure gluttony, morning, noon, and night.

HEIRLOOM VARIETIES—OLD-TIME FAVORITES

If you have the chance to grow your own fruits and vegetables, there is a lot you can expect. First of all, do a little research and find out which varieties you would most like to cultivate. It's essential that you taste what you want to plant and grow. The disappointment can be great—and I speak from bittersweet experience—when you take a bite of a pear that you have been waiting for and it tastes just ordinary and humble, not unlike what you can buy in the supermarket.

In the old days, country varieties were part of our agriculture system. Farmers bred their own varieties, year after year, by preserving the best tubers and seeds. This meant farmers always had a constant supply of healthy and resistant plant

NATURE WAS NEVER DESIGNED TO MEET THE DEMANDS WE MAKE ON IT TODAY

varieties that did well in their area. Because of this, old heirloom varieties often contain the greatest amount of genetic variation, which bestows several unique properties, including texture, color, form, taste, nutrients, and resistant genes—the more resistant genes a plant contains, the more bitter substances it will have—all of which are developed in and by nature. The modern agriculture industry doesn't use heirloom varieties, because their yield fluctuates, and is often too low. Modern fruits and vegetables are processed in many ways, and especially to produce high yields, but most of the varieties we know today were bred from the genetic variations of the country varieties. Over time, industry made them sweeter and sweeter—and milder and milder. The healthy bitter substances that you find in the old country varieties, especially in root vegetables and cabbage, were rejected in favor of a uniform range of flavor and aroma, with a more jovial taste and scent profile. And that is a shame, because the bitter substances are healthy, and contain sharp, peppery notes that make food far more interesting. Fortunately, those of us with gardens have the freedom to grow exactly what we want, and luckily, heirloom varieties are relatively easy to get hold of, either as seeds on the Internet, or as plants and tubers from passionate growers. And if you're interested in health, phenomenal taste, varied shapes, and irresistible colors, you can be glad that more and more skilled farmers are choosing to work with the old country varieties. They are often available from better food shops, direct farm sales, and local food markets.

GROWING FAST VS. GROWING SLOW

Regardless of which ingredient or food product is cultivated, if it is grown quickly, there will be a reduction in quality that will affect the aroma, taste, and texture. Nevertheless, fruit and vegetable varieties that can be grown quickly—and grown large—are in demand. To achieve this, nitrogen (liquid manure) or chemical fertilizers (non-organic) are often used. The downside is that fruits and vegetables that are given too much nitrogen lack character, precisely because they are not fully developed, even if they look big, juicy, and beautiful on the outside. Their texture will be looser, while their smell and taste will be poor, heavy, and awkward. They actually smell like farts when they are cooked—sorry, but there is no better word to describe it! Watering is another method that is used, particularly with large greenhouse plants, to achieve high yields in a short time. Water does help plants grow, but too much water leaves behind an immature and anonymous taste, even if the fruits and vegetables appear ripe and ready to eat. For instance, the more water a tomato gets, the larger and heavier it becomes, and thus the more money the farmer—or corporation—can charge. But, all that extra water only waters down the tomato's natural flavors. Fruits and vegetables grown with farmyard manure, compost, or organic fertilizer grow more slowly, and have time to develop more character. They're more expressive, balanced, and mature, and acquire greater resistance, which generates more healthy bitter substances inside the plants, as well as better texture and more sweetness.

APPEARANCES ARE DECEPTIVE

The storage methods used have an enormous effect on the texture, taste, and shelf life of fruits and vegetables. I prefer mine to be unwashed, because they're protected by a thin layer of soil that acts like packaging, helping to retain valuable flavors and nutrients. And if you ask any grower, their answer will be the same as mine. Today, most potatoes and root vegetables are sold washed and often polished, which reduces both taste and durability, but makes them incredibly easy to cook. The polishing scratches the skin, which is their natural packaging. If they're kept in a place that's too warm, as they always are in supermarkets—and wrapped in plastic, too—they naturally begin to perspire. These are ideal conditions for producing mold, rot, and sprouting, but if we can't be bothered to rinse lettuce or scrub a potato, it's our own fault.

MEANWHILE, IN THE FOREST...

Out in the wild, plants put down roots in places where they'll thrive and get what they need: water, sunlight, and nutrients. A seed sprouts where it lands, or else it does not. Nature was never designed to meet the demands we make on it today. Natural plants need no outside help from fertilizers or chemical pesticides in order to thrive. When their season is over, they wither. Meanwhile, other plants emerge in the woods, on the shore, and along the wild hedges. Wildlife moves freely and finds its own sustenance. The same goes for fish and shellfish. In this way, the flora and fauna of a region have time to leave their mark on the scent, taste, and texture of ingredients. As a result, food gathered in the wild often contains more unique flavors and nutrients than the cultivated plants and farmed animals and fish we can buy in the stores.

PICKED FROM THE BERRY BUSHES

LEMON JUICE / TARRAGON / CANE SUGAR / SPEARMINT / BRONZE FENNEL FLOWERS

GOOSEBERRY

ICE-COLD GOOSEBERRY LEMONADE

400 g (14 oz) gooseberries

CHARACTER

Intense, fresh, and warm, with subtle bitterness, a summer attitude, creamy pollen notes, and elegant herbal delight.

VARIATIONS

The aromatic blend can also be used with raspberries, strawberries, black currants, blackberries, peaches, or melons. Or, it can be diluted and enjoyed just as it is (without added fruit).

AROMATIC BLEND #47

250 g (9 oz) light cane sugar
100 ml (7 tbsp) freshly squeezed lemon juice
5 g (1/6 oz) fresh tarragon
5 g (1/6 oz) fresh spearmint, plus more for topping
10 g (1/3 oz) fresh bronze fennel flowers

Approx. 2 l (2 qt) ice-cold water for serving

This lemonade is refreshing and elegant, but has an extremely wild flavor. Gooseberries are my favorite berries, because they're exotic and they possess a unique balance of sweetness and tartness. They must be ripe, with skin so transparent that you can see the seeds inside; otherwise, you'll go to a lot of trouble for nothing. Bronze fennel blooms in late July. The orange-yellow pollen contains crazy, delightful notes of warm fennel. If you cannot get hold of the flowers, replace them with ordinary fennel. Or, increase the amount of tarragon and spearmint. Finally, remember that small ice cubes will quickly dilute the lemonade, and weaken the overall taste. A large piece of ice will not do this, so freeze 480 ml (2 cups) of water in a bag then chop off big chunks and drop them into glasses for serving. That way, the ice will serve its proper purpose, which is to cool the drink, without diluting it too much. The concentrate is best served on the day it is made.

AROMATIC BLEND

Put the light cane sugar and lemon juice in a small saucepan and bring to a boil. Continue boiling until the sugar is dissolved. Add the tarragon, spearmint, and fennel flowers then cover with a lid and turn off the heat. Keep hot. Durability: 2 weeks in the refrigerator. Makes 240 ml (1 cup).

GOOSEBERRIES

Put the gooseberries in a medium bowl (there is no need to pinch off the tops) and add the hot aromatic blend. (Heat brings out the gooseberries' aroma, so it is important that the aromatic blend be hot; otherwise, you'll end up with a completely different flavor.) Let cool completely at room temperature then purée in a food processor or blender, and pour through a fine-mesh sieve; discard the solids. Store the concentrate in the refrigerator up to 1 week. When serving, mix 50 ml (3 1/4 tbsp) concentrate with 100–150 ml (7–10 tbsp) ice-cold water. Put a large chunk of ice in a glass, pour the lemonade over, and, if desired, add a couple spearmint leaves.

SEASON: June–August
Drinks for 12
Makes 600 ml (2½ cups) concentrate

THAI BASIL / COCONUT MILK / TAPIOCA PEARLS / BITTER ALMOND / CANE SUGAR / ALMOND MILK

RASPBERRY

RASPBERRY PUDDING

250 g (9 oz) ripe raspberries, plus more for topping

CHARACTER

An exotic blend with a delightful gelatinous texture, elegant almond aromas, and quiet fragrant basil notes.

VARIATIONS

The aromatic blend can also be used with strawberries, blackberries, blueberries, and cherries, or sliced fruit, such as peaches and apricots.

AROMATIC BLEND #48

480 ml (2 cups) almond milk or whole milk
200 ml (13 tbsp) coconut milk (min. 80% coconut)
60 g (2 oz) tapioca pearls
50 g (3½ tbsp) light cane sugar
1 (1 g) finely grated bitter almond (optional) (see p. 277)
30 (10 g) fresh Thai basil leaves

Tapioca pearls are made of starch extracted from cassava or yucca root. Throughout Asia and South America, the pearls are used as a thickening agent—like cornstarch and potato starch—for various dishes, including much-loved tapioca pudding. There are several reasons why I love this starch, especially the pearls. It's gluten-free, easy to work with, and unlike some other starches, it can be boiled. It also has an exotic, transparent look, an adorable wobbly texture, and a taste that's pure and discreetly sweet. Whenever I make tapioca pudding, it puts me in a good mood, and in an instant I'm back in Shanghai, where I first tasted it. Buy tapioca pearls that are not labeled "instant" or "precooked".

AROMATIC BLEND

Put the almond milk, coconut milk, tapioca pearls, light cane sugar, and bitter almond, if using, in a small saucepan and bring to a boil. Reduce the heat and simmer, stirring constantly to prevent burning, for 20–30 minutes, or until the pearls are completely transparent and the texture is thick, gelatinous, and wobbly. During the last 5 minutes of cooking, add the Thai basil. Turn off the heat. Durability: Use immediately. Makes 800 ml (3⅓ cups).

RASPBERRIES

Spread the raspberries and the warm pudding in alternating layers in 4 bowls or glasses. The pudding can be served hot, warm, or ice-cold, topped with more raspberries. To serve ice-cold, press plastic wrap directly on the surface of the pudding to prevent a film from developing, and refrigerate at least 2 hours.

SEASON: June–October
Dessert for 4

BLACK PEPPER / APPLE CIDER VINEGAR / HONEY / EDIBLE FLOWERS

STRAWBERRY

STRAWBERRIES AND FLOWERS

600 g (21 oz) ripe strawberries

CHARACTER
A feminine and sophisticated blend with sweet, dominant floral notes from the pollen dust and subtle fruity sharpness.

VARIATIONS
The aromatic blend can also be used with most berries and fruits. It can be served, with or without yogurt, as a sweetener with your morning muesli.

AROMATIC BLEND #49
130 g (4 ½ oz) honey
30 ml (2 tbsp) unfiltered apple cider vinegar
5 g (⅛ oz) fresh edible flowers, plus more for topping
A pinch of freshly ground black pepper

A handful of fresh basil leaves (topping)
150 ml (10 tbsp) heavy cream (topping)

This is a gentle but sophisticated way to give strawberries—or any of summer's many delicate berries—a warm exotic touch. You can make the aromatic blend with any flower that's full of pollen dust and has a hint of charming sweetness, such as deep blue lavender or sage flowers, orange marigold, creamy elderflowers, purple spearmint blossom, pink scented rose petals, and those intensely fragrant bronze fennel flower umbels. The aromatic blend is best when used hot.

AROMATIC BLEND
Put the honey and apple cider vinegar in a small saucepan and bring to a boil then immediately turn off the heat. Add the flowers (5 g / 50 ml) and the freshly ground black pepper and let stand for 15 minutes before using. You can strain the aromatic blend or leave the flowers in when using. Keep hot. Durability: 4–6 days at room temperature. Makes 120 ml (½ cup).

STRAWBERRIES
Pinch off and discard the tops of the strawberries and cut the fruit into quarters or slices. To serve, toss the strawberries with the fresh flowers and basil leaves then add the hot aromatic blend, followed by the cream.

SEASON: June–July
Snack or dessert for 4

WHEAT FLOUR/SEA SALT FLAKES/ALLSPICE/EGG/ STAR ANISE/CHOCOLATE/ BUTTER/ANCHO CHILI/ CANE SUGAR

BLACK CURRANT

BLACK CURRANT BROWNIES

200 g (7 oz) fresh black currants

CHARACTER

A slightly smoky, dark, masculine, and rich blend with subtle notes of warm chili and star anise.

VARIATIONS

The aromatic blend can also be used with various nuts, cereals (rye flakes, wheat flakes, oats, and spelt), freeze-dried or fresh berries, and diced fruit.

AROMATIC BLEND #50

175 g (6 ¼ oz) dark chocolate (min. 85%), roughly chopped
150 g (5 ¼ oz) unsalted butter
3 g (1 tsp) ancho chili flakes (see p. 65)
2 (2 g) whole star anise
10 (1.5 g) whole allspice berries
4 medium eggs
500 g (18 oz) light cane sugar
2 g (½ tsp) sea salt flakes
150 g (5 ¼ oz) plain wheat flour

Filling, wonderful, and thoroughly unhealthy—these brownies should be eaten in moderation, as a piece of confectionery. They're at their very best after two days, but will keep for a week. When sun-ripened black currants are out of season, they can easily be replaced with other berries or diced fruit. Just make sure the fruit has plenty of acidity and a sharp taste. If it's too sweet, the contrast between the dark aromatic blend and the fruit is not interesting enough. You can use any chili flakes you like, but the smoky flavor from the ancho chili flakes does make a difference.

AROMATIC BLEND

In a bowl set over a water bath, gently heat the chocolate and butter until melted. Put the ancho chili flakes, star anise, and allspice berries in an electric coffee grinder and grind to a fine powder. Stir the powder into the chocolate and butter mixture. Meanwhile, beat the eggs, light cane sugar, and sea salt flakes in a large bowl until foaming. Add the melted chocolate mixture to the egg mixture, whisking quickly and strongly, preferably with an electric whisk, until smooth. Add the flour and whisk until smooth. Durability: Use immediately. Makes 1.2 l (5 cups).

BLACK CURRANTS

Fold the black currants (if using fresh black currants, there is no need to pinch off the tops) into the aromatic blend and pour into a parchment paper–lined baking pan (23 x 32 x 5 cm / 9 x 12 x 2 in). Bake in a preheated 190° C (375° F) oven for 10 minutes, or until the top has a shiny, papery crust and the sides are just beginning to come away from the pan. Allow the brownies to cool completely then refrigerate until cold. Cut the brownies into thin slices and serve ice-cold, straight from the refrigerator.

SEASON: July–August
Dessert or snack for 16

THE ESSENTIALS OF HERBS & SPICES

I'm a romantic—there's no doubt about it. But I'm not so sentimental that I add spices simply to evoke memories of the countries I've traveled to, or those I've dreamed of visiting. My focus, or obsession, if you like, is strictly to highlight and enhance the taste of ingredients with the help of herbs and spices. Why? Because herbs and spices contain the highest concentration of aromatic substances that can be found in plants. Over the next few pages, I describe some of the seasonings I've worked with over the past twenty years, but it's really the amount of aromatic substances in a given herb or spice that has the greatest impact on how you experience it. So grab a seed, close your eyes, and crush it slightly between your teeth. Wait, sense, and observe. This should give you a reasonable idea of what awaits. For the next half hour, you'll taste all manner of aromatic compounds (essential oils) that will unfold, and create sensory experiences in your mouth. It's a really good exercise. Actually, it's one of the best ways to evaluate the aromatic potential of a spice you've just purchased, or are considering buying. One thing that time and my work has taught me is that you can't trust blindly in herbs and spices. Use your nose and your taste buds—they won't mislead your eyes.

GRAB A SEED, CLOSE YOUR EYES, AND CRUSH IT SLIGHTLY BETWEEN YOUR TEETH. WAIT, SENSE, AND OBSERVE

QUALITY

You can find some of the finest and most interesting herbs and spices when traveling and visiting local food markets. Keep an eye out for local wild spices in particular. Never buy the powdered versions, no matter how attractively they're presented. You have no way of knowing how fresh they are, or what else they may contain. Instead, choose whole spices that have been grown without pesticides or chemical fertilizers, and seek out those that are certified organic or biodynamic. Serious health food stores will offer a wide range, but nowadays you can find most of them, especially the more exotic ones, online. Whole spices should look appetizing, even if you don't know what to do with them. You should be able to feel the freshness just by touching them, or by opening the lid of the jar. If they have a lively aroma, you're ready to go into the kitchen.

ALLSPICE
Pimenta dioica L.

The unique aspect of this spice is that it smells and tastes of several spices at once, hence the name 'allspice.' It's like a combination of cloves, nutmeg, cinnamon, and pepper. If you get hold of fine allspice berries, you'll experience warm, spicy, smoky notes, followed by a short, sharp pepper flavor. Allspice is, without a doubt, one of my favorite spices, because it can be added to almost anything, both sweet and savory.

ANISE SEEDS
Pimpinella anisum

Anise is the darling of the food industry, because it contains a fine licorice flavor that's cheaper than licorice root. It also has the ability to mask undesirable tastes in medicine. Anise is feisty, hot, and spicy, with a hint of star anise. If you compare anise seeds with fennel seeds, anise is creamier and milder in flavor.

BAY LEAVES
Laurus nobilis

I only use fresh bay leaves, because they are less strong and more aromatic than the dried ones. What's more, I have two large bay leaf shrubs that provide me with an ample supply all year round. I strongly recommend getting a bay leaf plant. Small ones take up very little space and they're an inexpensive way to always have fresh bay leaves on hand. Fresh bay leaves have a medicinal quality that can best be described as an attractive pine attitude, with a hint of cooling camphor and notes of citrus and green grass. If the leaves are boiled for too long, all this disappears. Try rolling the fresh leaves tightly together, cutting them first into very thin strips, and then chopping them very finely—it can never be too fine. After a few minutes of cooking—or a little longer—you'll experience much more of bay leaf's elegant character.

BITTER ALMOND
Prunus dulcis var. amara

Almond trees produce both sweet and bitter almonds. Bitter almonds are interesting, because they contain many more aromatic compounds than the sweet ones. This means that a single bitter almond can quite quickly give a dish the characteristic marzipan attitude that most people love. It can be grated quickly and easily using a very fine rasp grater. The downside is that bitter almonds contain tiny amounts of the toxic compound amygdalin (a precursor to hydrogen cyanide), which can be harmful in large quantities. Don't be frightened by this, but be sure to carefully follow a recipe's specified amounts. In Sweden, where I live, bitter almonds are available in ordinary supermarkets, all year round. The same is true in Germany. They are not expensive and they make dishes extra interesting. In other countries, such as the United States, imports of bitter almonds are banned. There is no good alternative to bitter almond, so if you can't get hold of them, omit them from the recipe. There are also some interesting bitter substances contained in the skin of ordinary sweet almonds, so if you don't remove the skins, you'll experience more of the aromatic substances. At the start of the chapter I wrote that if you take a seed and taste it, you'll get a reasonable idea of what you can expect. Don't try this with bitter almond!

BLACK CARDAMOM PODS
Amomum subulatum

Many people, including me, are scared witless by the heavy, smoky aroma that surrounds this spice. Try opening a pod and tasting one of the seeds. They taste surprisingly sweet, mild, and a little minty, with a hint of balsamic eucalyptus notes. You could almost get addicted to them, as the taste is so lovely and strange. This spice gets its dominant smoky aroma from a primitive and traditional drying process that takes place over a bonfire of large, damp logs. That's why most of the smoky aromas stay firmly in the pod not the seed. Instead of throwing out the empty pods, try using them to flavor black tea.

BLACK PEPPERCORN
Piper nigrum L.

Black pepper is an iconic spice. The finest versions have a spicy, sharp, and masculine fragrance. The taste is relatively dry and spicy, followed by warm resin and a hint of wood. When pepper is distilled by steam, it has a characteristic perfume that doesn't include the sharp, strong taste of the aromatic compound piperine. If you like the fresh fragrance of pepper, but not its strong taste, add freshly ground black pepper only at the very end of cooking. The steam from the hot meal will help release pepper's aromatic compounds. Conversely, if pepper is added at the beginning, more of its aromatic substances will be released and its flavor will be stronger and more mature.

BROWN MUSTARD SEEDS
Brassica juncea

Brown and black (*B. nigra*) mustard seeds have a strong, pungent, and burning taste, with brief bitterness and almost no scent. They are far more aromatic than yellow mustard seeds. Brown and black mustard seeds are most interesting when not blended, but instead dry-roasted and used whole, which replaces the bitterness with nuttiness. You can read more about how to do this in 'How to maximize flavor' (p. 60).

CARAWAY
Carum carvi

Caraway is a slightly bitter seed that initially makes you think of rye. Then comes a warm, sweet, and persistent aroma. It is cleansing and may sting slightly on the tongue, but that quickly disappears. Caraway seeds seem rustic, with a hint of fresh hay, but they're also elegant and slightly spicy. It's one of the spices that greatly benefits from being dry-roasted, which boosts the aromatic substances and increases sweetness.

CHILI
Capsicum

You can read more about chili in 'How to maximize flavor' (p. 63).

CINNAMON

CASSIA CINNAMON
Cinnamomum cassia

The taste and smell of cassia cinnamon is dark, masculine, very spicy, warm, and slightly rough, with a hint of resin. When you turn up the seasoning and use large amounts of chili and soy, cassia cinnamon is in its element, precisely because it's so strange and exotic. Ceylon cinnamon has none of these qualities. The two are like night and day, so it's essential that you buy and use the appropriate cinnamon.

CEYLON CINNAMON
Cinnamomum zeylanicum

I am a real cinnamon snob—it's nothing new; I've been one for more than twenty years—and exclusively use true Ceylon cinnamon. The United Kingdom is one of the few places with an actual law banning the use of the term 'true cinnamon' for anything except Ceylon cinnamon. But irrespective of its name or place of origin, the finest cinnamon is so structurally fragile that it's reminiscent of Cuban cigars, which can be crumbled easily between your fingertips. It's feminine and delicate, with a taste and fragrance that are sweet and full-bodied, plus warm floral notes and a hint of camphor. Don't overuse cinnamon, as that will make it seem ordinary, no matter how fine the quality. If it starts to remind you of Christmas, you've added too much. Most importantly, true Ceylon cinnamon should never be confused with the rock-hard cinnamon sticks called cassia (*Cinnamomum cassia*).

CINNAMON LEAVES
Cinnamomum verum

Dried cinnamon leaves (p. 276) can bring something magical and fragrant to your food that's experienced as a warm, sweet, and spicy scent. The leaves share many characteristics with cassia, except the masculine attitude. Cinnamon leaves are extremely easy to use in cooking, as they are simply added whole. However, finding them can involve a bit of detective work. If you don't succeed, wait. Replacing them with cassia cinnamon will only lead to trouble.

CLOVE
Syzygium aromaticum

The taste, scent, and appearance of this spice are unique. Clove is hefty, with a sweet, warm, deep, and penetratingly spicy scent and flavor. It often leaves a burning, astringent sensation on the tongue. This is because cloves contain quite large amounts of aromatic compounds. It is not a spice to be added liberally.

CORIANDER SEEDS
Coriandrum sativum

Coriander seeds have a sweet and aromatic taste, with warm notes of wood, nuts, and orange, plus a hint of pepper. The seed are relatively mild, which makes them extremely easy to work with, though they can vary tremendously in flavor. In this, coriander seeds are a bit like fennel seeds—you never know whether you've bought a pig in a poke. This is why it's essential to taste the seeds before using them. Take a seed, crush it between your teeth, and assess it. If you sense a clumsy, pronounced bitterness, find other coriander seeds. This is another spice that benefits greatly from being dry-roasted, which boosts its aromatic substances and increases its sweetness.

CUBEB
Piper cubeba L.

This berry is dominated by bitterness, with a sharp, hot, and spicy taste that's accompanied by camphor notes and a marked pine attitude. Sometimes parallels can be drawn with the hot spicy scent and taste of allspice seeds.

CUMIN SEEDS
Cuminum cyminum

Cumin seeds have a spicy, deep, dry, and dusty taste, as well as warm, soft, and spicy scent notes. The seed's potential is enormous, making it just as universal as coriander seed. The bitter aftertaste can sometimes be too marked, but that may be elegantly soothed by dry-roasting, which also produces more sweetness.

FENNEL SEEDS
Foeniculum vulgare dulce

There are enormous differences in the flavor of fennel seeds. Some contain neither anise notes nor sweetness, but are strongly bitter. It is, therefore, essential to know what kind of seed you've got your hands on before you use it in your cooking. Take a seed, crush it between your teeth, and assess it. 'Dulce' means sweet, and that's precisely what you want to experience, along with warm notes of anise and licorice, and a hint of earth, pepper, and wood. Sometimes, the Latin name, *Foeniculum vulgare dulce*, is on the label, but it's usually omitted.

FENUGREEK SEEDS
Trigonella foenum-graecum L

The aroma of fenugreek is thought to be the essence of India—it's featured in most curry blends—but this versatile spice is used in kitchens around the world. The taste is similar to burnt caramel, with a bitterness that can vary enormously. The scent is herb-like and dominated by lovage notes. Fenugreek is associated with a quite powerful odor, because it contains the aromatic substance sotolon. The seeds should always be dry-roasted in a hot pan before being ground and used. Roasting helps moderate fenugreek's strong odor and bitterness, making it more useful. It's difficult to precisely describe the scent and taste of fenugreek, because it inevitably reminds me of curry dishes, so I won't even try.

GINGER
Zingiber officinale

I'm obsessed with small ginger roots that are so fresh, and contain so few fibers, that they don't need to be peeled, and in which the taste is perfumed and delicate rather than strong and dominant. Fresh ginger root from Peru and Uganda (not China) contains a lively sharpness that's not too severe. It has a hint of wood and grass, accompanied by cooling eucalyptus and floral notes, and conveys a sense of purity and well-being. This is why fresh ginger mingles so well with so many different ingredients. When grating or chopping fresh ginger, do so across the grain. This makes the work easier, because the root doesn't shred as much. You can read more about how to vary the strength of fresh ginger in 'How to maximize flavor' (p. 60).

GREEN CARDAMOM PODS
Elettaria cardamomum

This is the world's third most expensive spice, and my absolute favorite. Genuine Indian Malabar cardamom (small round capsules) and Mysore cardamom (large oval and triangular capsules)

contain excellent aromatic compounds. What you pay a lot of money for is an exclusive and very feminine experience, full of cleansing, fresh notes of eucalyptus, camphor, and citrus. The fragrance is nearly identical, with additional notes of tropical timber. Don't be misled by the color: a fine green hue is not synonymous with high quality or a host of aromatic substances. As always, use your nose and your taste buds; they won't mislead your eyes. If you don't use the pods whole, remove the cardamom seeds before you put them in the mortar for grinding. Alternatively, put the whole pods in an electric coffee grinder and blend them. If the pods are blended alone, it can be difficult to pulverize them. Try adding a pinch of sea salt or sugar cane, depending on what the spice is to be used for, and, *voilà*, you have a uniform, white spice that's as finely ground as powdered sugar.

JUNIPER
Juniperus communis L.

Juniper immediately makes me think of winter and wild, rugged natural beauty. The taste starts out quite strong and refreshing, after which you experience significant pine notes. Juniper is dominant; it creates a slight burning sensation on the tongue, and has a brief bitterness. The scent is very similar. Incidentally, fresh, sun-ripened juniper berries, taken straight from the bush, before being dried, possess a resoundingly good prune-plum flavor. They can be used for the same purposes as dried juniper.

LEMON GRASS
Cymbopogon citratus

The lemon grass stem has a warm, quiet, and sweet lemon taste. The scent is subtle, albeit very feminine and delicate, with notes of grass, ginger, and roses, plus a hint of earth. The entire plant smells and tastes good, but it is the lower, white part of the root that contains the best aromas. It takes a little time to get the flavor out of lemon grass. Remove the dry, outermost leaves from the lemon grass. Trim the root, leaving it intact as much as possible, then use only 5 cm (2 in) of the lower, white part, and discard or reserve the dry green top. Use a pestle or the handle of a knife to crush the lower, white part then finely chop it or grind it in a mortar until you get an even, fine texture. The green top can be used in tea, soups, lemonades, and ice cream bases.

LONG PEPPER
Piper longum L.

This is an unusual spice in many ways. It looks like small, elongated conical fruits. And it's almost impossible to distinguish the scent from the taste, because it's all so different and strange. As a spice, long pepper is hot, even though it contains notes of cooling camphor. At first, it's bitter, but that's quickly replaced by an unusually sweet and full-bodied fragrance, along with balsamic notes of menthol and a hint of tropical wood. That may sound crazy, but as I said, this is an unusual spice. Long pepper has a relatively long-lasting and penetrating sharpness, and should be used with caution. However, once you get to know long pepper, you may find it quite irresistible.

LOOMI
Citrus aurantifolia

Dried lime, also known as loomi, lumi, or Oman lemon, is used in Middle Eastern cuisine, and has its origins in Persia. The small, light-brown limes (or lemons) are sun dried for a long time, and possess an intensely sour, hot flavor and aroma. They're a fantastic boon for dishes that cry out for the complex, fermented citrus notes that no other fruit can provide. To get access to this world of incredible flavor, the rock-hard, feather-light balls must be crushed with the palm of your hand or something heavy, and ground before they can be used. Another option is to simply puncture the loomi, and use them whole in slow-cooked dishes. If you're unsure, grind them to a fine powder in an electric coffee grinder. Store the lime powder in a sealed container, and any time a dish lacks that essential tartness, add a little of the powder. That way you can get to know the taste better, if you've never tried it before (p. 110).

NIGELLA
Nigella sativa

Also called black caraway, black cumin, fennel flower, Roman coriander, or *kalonji*, these blacks seeds resemble sesame seeds, but are five-sided in form. Nigella is an interesting and unusual spice. The taste is rich, spicy, and hot, with notes of mild pepper and cumin, plus a hint of oregano. The seed is neither ordinary nor insistent, and has an elegant herbal attitude. If the seed is exposed to heat, the taste becomes much stronger.

NUTMEG AND MACE
Myristica fragrans

Nutmeg is intensely aromatic, sweet, deep, and warm in taste. Sometimes you may even experience notes of smoke and wood. The dried nutmeg aril, known as mace, contains similar notes, but is milder, sweeter, and softer in flavor, with a hint of cinnamon. This makes mace more expensive than nutmeg, but it's worth the extra cost. As both nutmeg and mace contain large amounts of aromatic compounds, it doesn't pay to buy them in powdered form. Dried mace resembles dark yellow—or red if it's completely fresh—coarse fishing net, and can easily be chopped on a cutting board or ground in a mortar.

SAFFRON
Crocus sativus

Saffron is like a fine, expensive perfume, so you won't find any cheap saffron on the market. Either you buy the real thing, or you buy something else that resembles it. Genuine saffron should not be more than a year old. It brings an intense feminine power to food. The taste and fragrance are delicate, exclusive, graceful, deep, warm, and floral, with faint bitterness and dominant sweetness.

SMOKED PAPRIKA
Pimentón de la Vera

If you don't have access to a grill, you can use the Spanish smoked paprika called 'La Vera' paprika. This powdered spice has a warm, sweet, and mellow smoky taste, with a hint of fruit. The peppers are not sun-dried, but are traditionally smoked over oak for several weeks. Smoked paprika is available in sweet, mild, and strong versions. It is a Spanish specialty, and stamped Denominación de Origen from the La Vera region. To me, smoked paprika is a kind of magic, because every time I use it, I think of real wood, barbecues, and smoky bacon and that makes me very happy. I wouldn't call this spice refined, but it offers a quick and easy way to give all sorts of dishes a light smoky taste without having to use a grill.

STAR ANISE
Illicium verum

Star anise is similar to anise seed, cassia, clove, and licorice root, but with an even more masculine and dramatic scent and taste. Strange, exotic, and insistent, it should be used in moderation. Star anise creates a slightly 'dirty' but interesting licorice-like sweetness that goes especially well with spicy dishes.

SUMAC
Rhus coriaria

Sumac is another favorite in my kitchen. It comes from the dried, rust-red seeds of a fruit native to the Mediterranean, and is often available as a moist red powder. The taste is acidic, with a pronounced fruitiness that is less tart than lemon or vinegar. Sumac has the great advantage of not being a messy liquid, but rather a dry powder that can be sprinkled over all sorts of dishes to give them an elegant sharpness.

TURMERIC ROOT
Curcuma longa

I'm head over heels in love with turmeric root. And I'm not the only one. My adoration isn't for health reasons, but because tumeric is so wild and complex. Fresh turmeric root smells and tastes of orange, with notes of wood and pepper, plus a hint of ginger. It's also quite warming, and offers a hint of bitterness. The latter is mainly experienced if you use too much, especially in dishes that aren't heated. Turmeric's orange color is charming but also annoying, because it rubs off on the cutting board, your fingers, etc. When turmeric is dried, its most interesting aromatic substances disappear and it becomes more medicinal, dusty, and spicy.

MENUS FOR THE FOUR SEASONS

SPRING

(March / April / May)

144   Boiled asparagus
98   Gravlax
246   Chilled rhubarb soup

72   Celeriac curry
134   Juicy braised beef brisket
214   Featherlight seed cookies

FALL

(September / October / November)

156   Deep-fried fennel fritters
80   Smoky caramelized pumpkin
130   Pork preserved in apple jelly
260   Raspberry pudding

148   Grilled beans
52   Chard gratin
210   Flower yogurt

SUMMER

(June / July / August)

194   Summer flatbread chapatis
106   Grilled squid salad
230   Perfumed peach sorbet

76   Summer mashed potatoes
152   Juicy and creamy cucumber salad
118   Baked flattened chicken
264   Strawberries & flowers

WINTER

(December / January / February)

40   Crisp Salad of bitter endives
122   Fried and marinated duck breast
226   Deep-fried aromatic apple fritters

84   Pan-fried salsify
126   Glazed lamb meatballs
206   Fruit salami de luxe
242   Quince toddy

ABOUT THE PHOTOGRAPHS

Most people build a greenhouse to grow plants in. I made mine like a photo studio, as an extension of my atelier and just as tall and long. That means I can stand outside, under glass, all year round, and take photographs in daylight. The door of the greenhouse opens directly onto my kitchen. This is where all the recipes for this book were developed, from January to November 2016. Most of the vegetables, fruits, and herbs that you see I grew myself. They were harvested when they were in season—ripe and full of flavor. Perhaps you can even sense this from the photographs. Almost without exception, the photographs of my garden were taken at dusk. This is my favorite time of day: It's quiet, there are long, low shadows, and the sun's warm glow dapples the plants with varying hues. Shooting at this time allows my garden to be more fully experienced, so it's just as enchanting as it is in reality.

THANK YOU

To Morten

First of all, I want to thank my publisher, Christian Rieker from Prestel Verlag, whose belief in me and my work I appreciate so very much. I had the great fortune to work with Claudia Staeuble, my editor in chief on this project. This book was not easy, in all sorts of ways, and I want to express special and heartfelt thanks for Claudia's invaluable guidance and commitment. I have to thank Lauren Salkeld for being both gentle and sharp in her copy-editing of the English master. And, of course, enormous thanks go to Jack Dahl from Homework for providing us with the principle graphic layout. I'm also grateful to Hannah Feldmeier for typesetting the book with refinement. My thanks go to Carsten Seidel for his generosity in shooting the portraits for the book. I'm indebted to Antony Worrall Thompson and Chad Robertson for kindly contributing to the book and for all the shared moments in the past that still, to this day, affect me. I would like to thank Dennis Paphitis for spending time with me in New York, and taking me to the markets in Paris, where we cooked together. I did most of the work in the kitchen, but Dennis provided challenging questions for our interview. Finally, thanks to Morten, my husband, for his everlasting support in the background.

INDEX

A

Allspice berries, 83, 125, 133, 137, 209, 229, 241, 271
    basics, 277
Almond, bitter, 151, 233, 263
    basics, 277
Almond milk, 263
Almonds, 151, 209
Anise seeds, 101, 159, 233
    basics, 277
Apple juice, 43, 97, 109, 133, 245
Apples, 31
    Deep-fried aromatic apple fritters, 229
Aquavit or vodka, 115, 209
Aromatic blends
    questions and answers, 12, 15
    table of, 24–25
Asparagus
    Boiled asparagus, 147

B

Bacon, 55, 175
Barberries, 155
Basil, 79, 121, 263, 267
Bay leaves, 133, 137, 179
    basics, 277
Beans, dried
    Fragrant chickpea soup, 189
    Quick aromatic lentil soup, 201
Beans, grilled green or purple, 151
Beef
    Beef, juicy braised brisket, 137
Bergamot, 163
Bok choy
    Sweet and sour sautéed bok choy, 39
Brussels sprouts
    Warm Brussels sprouts salad, 31
Butternut squash (or pumpkin)
    Smoky carmelized pumpkin, 83

C

Caraway seeds, 217
basics, 277
green, 63
Cardamom pods, 47, 55, 189, 201, 213, 249
basics, 277
green, 278
Carrots
    Glazed carrots, 71
Cashews, 75, 155

Cauliflower, 97
    Roasted cauliflower, 35
Celeriac
    Celeriac curry, 75
Chapatis
    Summer flatbread chapatis, 197
Chard
    Chard gratin, 55
Cheese
    feta, 55, 163, 175, 179
    Parmesan, 35, 171
Chicken
    Baked flattened chicken, 121
Chickpea
    Fragrant chickpea soup, 189
Chilis. *See also* Peppers, long
    chipotle, 121
    dried ancho, 109
    flakes, 16, 39, 65, 87, 163, 179, 201, 237, 271, 277
    fresh, 59, 93
    jalapeño, 205
    Scoville scale, 63, 65
Chive blossoms, 175
Chocolate, 209, 271
Cilantro, 59, 71, 93, 109
Cinnamon
    Ceylon vs. cassia, 16
    leaves, 163, 189, 278
    sticks, 55, 83, 109, 121, 129, 209, 229, 245, 277–278
Citrus fruit, aroma extracts from, 114
Cloves, 133, 209, 229, 245
    basics, 278
Coconut
    creamed, 47, 201
    flour, 75
    milk, 249, 263
    sugar, 109, 125, 175
Cookies
    Featherlight seed cookies, 217
Coriander seeds, 31, 35, 75, 129, 163, 201, 229
    basics, 278
    green, 63
Cubeb berries, 133, 278
Cucumber
    Juicy and creamy cucumber salad, 155
Cumin seeds, 31, 87, 93, 109, 129, 171, 179, 193, 201
    basics, 278
Currants
    Black currant brownies, 271

D

Dates, 43
Desserts
    Black currant brownies, 271
    Chilled rhubarb soup, 249
    Deep-fried aromatic apple fritters, 229
    Featherlight seed cookies, 217
    Flower yogurt, 213
    Fruit salami de luxe, 209
    Perfumed peach sorbet, 233
    Raspberry pudding, 263
    Strawberries & flowers, 267
Drinks
    Ice-cold gooseberry lemonade, 259
    Quince toddy, 245
Duck
    Fried and marinated duck breast, 125

E

Eggs
    Crisp-fried light and fluffy omelet, 193
Elderflowers, 39
Endive
    Crisp salad of bitter endives, 43

F

Fennel
    Deep-fried fennel fritters, 159
Fennel flowers, 171, 259
Fennel seeds, 51, 55, 79, 93, 101, 129, 137, 151, 171, 179
    basics, 278
    green, 63
Fenugreek seeds, 75, 137, 151, 171
    basics, 278
Feta, 55, 163, 175, 179
Fish and seafood
    Creamy mussel soup, 97
    Gravlax, 101
    Grilled squid salad, 109
    Pan-fried shrimp salad, 105
    Whole roasted mackerel, 93
Fish sauce (nuoc mam or nam pla), 59
Flavor
    tips for maximizing, 60–65
    unusual combinations, 113
Flower waters, 222, 233, 249
Flowers, edible, 197, 267
    basics, 220, 222–223
    bronze fennel, 171, 259
    chive blossoms, 175
    elderflowers, 39
    growing your own, 183

hibiscus, 105, 213, 223, 237
lavender, 213, 223
roses, 197, 222–223, 249
in yogurt, 213
Fruit, dried
    Fruit salami de luxe, 115, 209

G

Gardens
    homegrown luxury, 250, 253
    Swedish country, 182–183
Garlic, 31, 35, 59, 93, 105, 109, 163, 189, 201, 205
Ginger
    basics, 278
    fresh, 31, 47, 51, 62, 151, 193, 201, 205, 278
    ground, 229
Golden syrup, 179, 217
Gooseberries
    Ice-cold gooseberry lemonade, 259
Grapes, 241
Gravlax, 101

H

Hazelnuts, 83
Heirloom fruits and vegetables, 250, 253
Herbs
    dried, 274
    fresh, 62–63, 137, 183
Hibiscus flowers, 105, 213, 223, 237
Honey, 121, 220, 222, 267
Horseradish, 75, 97

J

Juniper berries, 55, 125, 133, 241, 245
    basics, 278

K

Kale
    Creamy and crunchy kale, 47
Kohlrabi
    Crisp raw kohlrabi salad, 51
Kumquats, 205

L

Lamb
    Glazed lamb meatballs, 129
Lamb's ear salad, 241
Lavender flowers, 213, 223
Leeks
    Silky fragrant leeks, 163
Lemon grass, 93, 105
    basics, 278–279
Lemon juice, 31, 39, 75, 83, 87, 163, 167, 233, 241, 259
Lemon verbena, 147
Lemon zest, 39, 101, 151, 163

Lentil
   Quick aromatic lentil soup, 201
Lime juice, 59, 121
Loomi (dried lime), 71, 113, 121
   basics, 279

M
Mace. *See* Nutmeg or mace
Mackerel
   Whole roasted mackerel, 93
Main dishes
   Baked flattened chicken, 121
   Glazed lamb meatballs, 129
   Juicy braised beef brisket, 137
   Whole roasted mackerel, 93
Maple syrup, 83, 179, 229
Melon
   Melon salad, 237
Menus, seasonal, 281
Mint. *See also* Spearmint
Mussel
   Mussel soup, 97
Mustard seeds
   brown, 75, 147, 171, 179, 277
   gray, 62
   roasting, 62

N
Nigella seeds, 31, 159, 171, 179
   basics, 279
Nutmeg or mace, 31, 35, 75, 83,
   129, 163
   basics, 279
   green, 63

O
Oils, selecting, 19
Onion, 31, 87, 129, 179, 241
   Grilled onion salad, 167
Orange blossom water, 233
Orange zest, 245
Oranges, blood, 51
Oregano, 109, 167, 241

P
Paprika
   sweet, 55, 129
   sweet smoked, 83, 137, 279
Parmesan, 35, 171
Parsley, 151
Peaches, 79
   Perfumed peach sorbet, 233
Peanuts, 59, 93
Pear
   Hot grilled pear salad, 241
Peppercorns, 55, 109, 137, 241
   basics, 277
   vs. chili flakes, 16

Peppers, long, 125, 133
   basics, 279
Pistachios, 47, 79, 209
Pollen, 222
Pollination, 220, 253
Pomegranate syrup, 129
Pomegranates, 87
Pork
   bacon, 55, 175
   Pork preserved in apple jelly, 133
Potatoes, 97
   Summer mashed potatoes, 79
Pots and pans, cast iron, 20
Poultry
   Baked flattened chicken, 121
   Fried and marinated duck breast,
   125
Pumpkin (or butternut squash)
   Smoky carmelized pumpkin, 79

Q
Quince
   Quince toddy, 245

R
Radishes, 39
   Radish salad, 175
Raspberry
   Raspberry pudding, 263
Rhubarb
   Chilled rhubarb soup, 249
Rice
   Sweet and sour rice, 205
Rosemary, 125, 245
Roses
   dried petals, 249
   flower water, 222, 249
   fresh petals, 197, 223, 249, 267
   rose oil, 222–223

S
Saffron, 43, 79, 97, 233
   basics, 279
Sage, 193
Salads
   Crisp raw kohlrabi salad, 51
   Crisp salad of bitter endives, 43
   Grilled onion salad, 167
   Grilled squid salad, 109
   Hot grilled pear salad, 241
   Juicy and creamy cucumber salad, 155
   Melon salad, 237
   Pan-fried shrimp salad, 105
   Radish salad, 175
   Roasted zucchini salad, 171
   Tomato salad, 179
   Warm Brussels sprout salad, 31

Salmon
   Gravlax, 101
Salsify
   Pan-fried salsify, 87
Scales, 19
Scoville scale, 63, 65
Sea salt, 16, 19
Seasonal ingredients, 63, 140–141
Sesame paste (tahini), 87
Shallots, 193, 201
Shrimp
   Pan-fried shrimp salad, 105
Side dishes. *See* Starter or side dishes
Snacks
   Deep-fried aromatic apple fritters,
   229
   Deep-fried fennel fritters, 159
   Flower yogurt, 213
   Fruit salami de luxe, 115, 209
   Strawberries & flowers, 267
   Summer flatbread chapatis, 197
Soups
   Chilled rhubarb soup, 249
   Creamy mussel soup, 97
   Fragrant chickpea soup, 189
   Quick aromatic lentil soup, 201
Spearmint, 31, 87, 129, 155, 175,
   259
Spices
   aromas, art of retaining, 60
   green, 63
   grinding, 62, 65
   quality, 274
   roasting, 19, 60, 62
   time as, 62
   whole vs. ground, 19
Spinach, 201, 205
   Quick sautéed spinach, 59
Squid
   Grilled squid salad, 109
Star anise, 205, 271
   basics, 279
Starter or side dishes. *See also* Salads
   Boiled asparagus, 147
   Celeriac curry, 75
   Chard gratin, 55
   Creamy and crunchy kale, 47
   Crisp-fried light and fluffy omelet, 193
   Fried and marinated duck breast, 125
   Glazed carrots, 71
   Gravlax, 101
   Grilled beans, 151
   Pan-fried salsify, 87
   Pork preserved in apple jelly, 133

   Quick sautéed spinach, 59
   Roasted cauliflower, 35
   Silky fragrant leeks, 163
   Smoky carmelized butternut
      pumpkin, 83
   Summer mashed potatoes, 79
   Sweet and sour rice, 205
   Sweet and sour sautéed bok choy, 39
Strawberry
   Strawberries & flowers, 267
Sumac, 147, 167
   basics, 279

T
Tahini (sesame paste), 87
Tarragon, 51, 97, 101, 147, 259
Tomatoes, 189, 201
   Tomato salad, 179
Toppings, 15
Treacle, black, 217
Turmeric
   basics, 279
   dried, 201
   fresh, 31, 75, 105, 179, 193, 279

V
Vanilla pods, 233
Vinegar, unfiltered apple cider, 39,
   105, 114–115, 133, 171, 205, 241,
   267
   basics, 19
Vodka or aquavit, 115, 209

W
Walnuts, 209
Whiskey, 115

Y
Yogurt, 31, 71
   Yogurt with flowers, 213

Z
Zucchini
   Roasted zucchini salad, 171

ABOUT
THE AUTHOR

Kille Enna is a trained chef, critically acclaimed cookbook author, botanical explorer, and self-taught photographer. In her 25-year career, she has made a name for herself as an expert in spices and organic food, with a focus on seasonal ingredients skillfully blended with exotic flavors. Originating from Denmark, Kille Enna lives and works in the countryside of Southern Sweden, where she composes premium botanical extracts in the Aroma Atelier she founded in 2015.

www.killeenna.com

© Prestel Verlag, Munich · London · New York 2017
A member of Verlagsgruppe Random House GmbH
Neumarkter Strasse 28 · 81673 Munich

In respect to links in the book, Verlagsgruppe Random House expressly notes that no illegal content was discernible on the linked sites at the time the links were created. The Publisher has no influence at all over the current and future design, content, or authorship of the linked sites. For this reason Verlagsgruppe Random House expressly disassociates itself from all content on linked sites that has been altered since the link was created and assumes no liability for such content.

Prestel Publishing Ltd.
14–17 Wells Street
London W1T 3PD

Prestel Publishing
900 Broadway, Suite 603
New York, NY 10003

A CIP catalogue record for this book is available from the British Library.

Photos, text, and recipes: Kille Enna
Portraits and photos p. 5, 14, 22, 251, 252:
Seidel Photography

Editorial direction Prestel: Claudia Stäuble
Copyediting: Lauren Salkeld
Design: Jack Dahl, homework
Layout: Hannah Feldmeier
Typesetting: Hilde Knauer
Production management: Corinna Pickart
Separations: Mohn Media
Printing and binding: Mohn Media Mohndruck GmbH, Gütersloh
Paper: Tauro

Verlagsgruppe Random House FSC® N001967

Printed in Germany

ISBN 978-3-7913-8283-8 (English edition)

www.prestel.com